FUNNY
HOW IT
WORKS
OUT

MANON MATHEWS

FUNNY
HOW IT
WORKS
OUT

PERSONAL STORIES & LESSONS
ON HOW I GOT MY SH*T TOGETHER

MASTERLESS
PRESS

www.masterlesspress.com

Masterless Press
www.masterlesspress.com

First Masterless Press print edition: July 2020

Printed in the United States of America

ISBN: 978-1-7350801-0-9 (print)
ISBN: 978-1-7350801-1-6 (ebook)
ISBN: 978-1-7350801-2-3 (Hardcover)

To my always encouraging parents
Terri & Temple Mathews.

CONTENTS

An Introduction

HELLO! AND WELCOME to *Funny How It Works Out!* Truth bomb time. Abrupt, I know. You ready? There's a lesson in each moment that passes, if you pay attention. From embarrassing myself as a child to shamefully blacking out in Vegas to blowing up on social media to a storybook-turned-drama movie marriage and my life now as a content-creating comedian, I'm sharing this collection of wacky and seemingly impossible but true stories from my life with you in hopes that you can learn from the lessons in each anecdote and take steps toward manifesting your best life with a peaceful state of mind using my roller coaster of experiences as an example.

Oh, and at the end of the book is a little bonus for you. It's just a collection of short life tips that I practice daily to keep me centered and on the right track. Call it free therapy for anyone who may need it. If you follow me @manonfestation on Instagram, you've probably heard some variation of them, but at least now you'll have them handy if your battery is low or the internet goes out... Am I right?

This won't be a tell-all about my Vine-famous life. Vine was only one chapter in the grand scheme of things that changed my journey, so I won't go heavy on it. And I may be internet famous to some, but I promise it isn't all glitz, glam, and good times that lie in the pages ahead. It's better! JK. By the end of this book, if you've smiled, laughed, cried, and shaken your head at me a few times on top of learning a thing or two (or six), then I've done my job.

Yippee!

This book is a reminder that I, like everyone who's made it big in the days of social media, am a flesh-and-blood human just like you. (Unless you're a dog; then we are a bit different. I'm less hairy. Okay, that's a lie. If I let myself go, I can look like Chewbacca's wife.) Sure, just because the right confluence of events occurred at the right time and I achieved some "stardom," it doesn't mean that I didn't have to work hard or take heart-pounding risks to get there. If you're someone who hasn't achieved your dreams yet, that doesn't mean you're not going to. (Spoiler alert—you can when you DECIDE to!) And you *WILL* so long as you put yourself out there, keep going, seize opportunity, and *listen* to what the universe or whatever higher power you believe in is telling you in every moment. Because there *are* signs if you know where to look. Like a sparrow flying into your head through your window while you're driving (which actually happened to me—more on that later).

Funny How It Works Out is a reminder that even those who have manifested their best lives are not without their fair share of obstacles. Take me for example. My family has a history of alcoholism, depression, and anxiety, not to mention schizophrenia and obesity… *Ha. Ha. Ha.* And the best part is, that's from both sides of the family! *Yay…*

For the record, I'm not schizo (*yet*), but I've had to do a lot to overcome the parts of those genetic hurdles that trickled into my coding—like my abusive Lifetime-movie relationship with my old flame, whom you may have heard of. Al Cohol? He's starred in movies such as *The Hangover, Project X,* and *Superbad,* and essentially made guest appearances in every movie ever. I had to learn how to focus on what's good in my life and to train my brain to be in the present moment, to attract good things, and to let the past go. The value of accomplishing all of that is what I hope to impart to you before the acknowledgments section.

Jess-ka: *"Gosh, Manon, I can't imagine what it's like having it all figured out!"*

Oh, honey, but I don't. I'm still learning, and I hope I never stop learning. May I remain teachable FOREVER.

Jess-ka: *"Yeah, but you've made it! You totally, like, ManonFested your best life! You must be so happy, like, all the time!"*

OH HELL NO. I mean, yes, I am grateful I get to do what I love for a living, but does that mean I'm always 100 percent happy where I am in life in all moments? No way! Ya know… not everything is as it appears. Especially on social media. It is an everyday conscious effort for me to live in the moment and to be comfortable with myself wherever I'm at. People tend to show only the pretty side of the coin online. I hope there will be a day when we are courageous enough to show it all. Hence, this is why I wrote this book. It's the other, NASTY side of my coin.

There are two things that I'm very proud of:

1.) I got a call to headline at Caroline's on Broadway in New York, and actually pulled it off.

2.) In the summer of 2019, I did an adult thing and bought a house in Los Angeles—the city where I was born and raised.

I know what you're thinking: *There are people who are actually from LA? Da fuq?*

Whenever I tell people that I'm from La-La Land, they look at me like I'm an alien (which I am NOT… but how would I know? Aren't we all aliens?). I get it; most people move to LA to pursue their dreams. But this is home for me, and not because it's my literal home. It's home because I know it so well. This is where I feel safe and where it feels like I truly belong. It's familiar, which makes it comfortable. We humans like to stay comfy, don't we? We spend our whole lives trying to keep safe and surround ourselves with familiar things. But I will say that the most fulfilled I've ever been was when I got *OUTSIDE* of my comfy zone and did something *NEW*.

Life takes abrupt turns. External factors pop up out of frigging nowhere and sometimes try to knock us off our path. *Cough*

COVID-19 *cough* Down spells come along even when you're riding high on the path you've always dreamed of walking. Good news is you're safe reading this book and your immune system is stronger than ever just because you picked it up ;).

Happiness? It's a fickle thing… Unless you *CHOOSE* otherwise. Which we can. Did you know that?! When I really truly KNEW that to my core, my whole world changed! Well, my perspective did. That's the goal here. That's what Marianne Williamson talks about in her lectures on *A Course in Miracles*: we just need to change our PERSPECTIVE of our situation, which is, in turn, called a MIRACLE! WOOOO, so magical! Marianne is amazing. She should carry a magic wand.

Thankfully, now that I have a solid grasp on the way that I think, I can get myself to a place where I am fully content at any time that I choose. Part of that I attribute to the fact that in 2015 I got my master certification as a neurolinguistic programming practitioner (NLP). Neurolinguistic programming, for those who don't know, is the study of language and how it affects the unconscious mind. Our unconscious mind is like a conductor that is always directing our conscious mind. And our conscious mind is like an orchestra playing whatever the conductor tells it to. Our unconscious mind is what controls our behavior. I don't think we realize just how powerful language is. Language is everything! Read that again… maybe even get a tattoo. Language is EVERYTHING. We must be diligent about what we say to ourselves and others. We are always listening. Even when we don't know it. Our unconscious is like a little kid who is always picking up info. It takes things very literally and doesn't have a sense of humor… much like my Grandma.

Sorry, Grandma, but you just didn't laugh at anything I did when I was a kid and I'm HILARIOUS.

It's okay, she won't read this since she's no longer with us… Or, as Marianne would say, "She's continued on…" Birth is not a beginning but a continuation, and the same goes with death. It's so refreshing to know that we don't have to freak about dying! Yay! We get to just enjoy our lives and dance around like monkeys! That's what I've tried to choose for most of my life—to dance and swing from the chandeliers.

Anyway… It was all those amazing lessons I learned in the stories I'm going to share with you that really allowed me to get where I am today. I'm a quiet, introverted, extroverted SUPER FREAK! And maybe you are too! Or maybe you're normal. What is normal? Maybe you're perfectly comfortable in your skin. Or maybe you're still figuring that out. Whatever you are is just PERFECT. I believe that we are pretty much all one and the same with a few minor details that make us unique! I don't know about you, but my deepest desire is to connect with myself, others, and my source. If that is true for you, then maybe you'll relate to some of the stories I share in this book.

1

Tinkle, Tinkle, Little Star

COMEDY, ACTING, MY lifelong dream of being a director—
sometimes I sit and think about what influenced me to pursue the
path I chose. Having hilarious and goofy parents definitely contributed
to that. I grew up watching shows like *Friends* and *Saturday Night Live*
and films like *Ace Ventura* and *The Mask*. I also obsessed over Robin
Williams (the funniest man ever to walk the planet), who was basically
my second father, though he didn't know it. And, as far as I know, he
never dated my mom. I sobbed for two weeks when he passed. Ouch,
hold on… I'm going to go cry now for a few minutes… Okay, I'm
back. One lesson I learned with his passing is that we must make sure
to make ourselves laugh first before sharing laughter with the world.

Growing up in LA and being so close to the film capital of the
world probably had something to do with my path, too. But after
sitting down and looking back, I think it was all of that and so much
more—like being the center of my parents' attention and royally
embarrassing myself—that probably served as the catalyst.

I was raised as an only child, so the focus was on me all of the time.
All of the time. ALL OF THE TIME! No breaks. Okay, except when I
was playing alone in my room, of course. I had ample time to be in the
mirror practicing faces and learning super cool Britney Spears and
NSYNC MTV VMA dances. I could have been a fantastic pop star.
And I still will be! You'll see, you'll all see!

The perk of having so much alone time as a kid was that it really
forced me to be creative. It allowed my imagination to soar. It's also

where I got a lot of my certainty from. Certainty, as Tony Robbins says, is one of the six basic human needs. We need certainty to feel safe and to function. So I had to find Wonder Woman strength within myself instead of getting validation from, let's say, siblings. I had to check in with myself first to see how *I* felt about something. Which means how *I* felt about anything that came to mind or anything I wanted to do mattered MOST. Now, that was great for the things I did well, but not so great for the things I didn't feel I did well. You see, I'm one of those people who feel like, if I can't do something wonderful and captivating, then WHY TRY? (Maybe you can relate?)

For instance, I loved singing. Back in ninth grade, I had to pick a song to sing in front of the whole classroom for a choir assignment. Umm, why did we have to do that?! That is such a terrifying thing to make a kid do. Dancing, fine... but singing?! That is SO vulnerable. For me. I chose Elton John's "Your Song" because I was OBSESSED with *Moulin Rouge*. I believe that the first time I heard Ewan McGregor sing that song, he imprinted on me, and later this made me choose the man I would marry, who looks just like him and is even Scottish like Ewan. Mr. McGregor was so impossibly dreamy, and his voice melted my heart. I would sing those songs all around the house and make myself cry.

Since my dad worked from home, he was the audience I practiced my choir performance for.

"You know, you're a better dancer than you are a singer," he said, his voice tinged with sarcasm.

Now, I know he didn't mean anything harsh by that. That was just his sense of humor. But self-conscious fourteen-year-old me took that in and internalized it, making it a story in my head that *my singing is just okay, not good ENOUGH*. The soul-crushing blow to my self-esteem turned into a decision not to pursue singing even though I loved it so much. I still do. I've created a new story in my head that I sound beautiful when I sing and that it doesn't need to be perfect.

It's a good thing that I had more than one dream. Becoming an actor was another. My parents kind of ignored that dream, though. I think they wanted to protect me and make sure that I had a normal childhood. In hindsight, I'm really grateful about that decision, because I got to have a wonderful childhood of anonymity and privacy and joy and freedom. (Thanks, guys! I owe ya one!) The way that I grew up is the reason I feel very serene in the world today, and that's just a gift, to feel like I'm with my people. With *you*.

My dad was one of those parents who was always filming home movies, so as the only child in the house and his firstborn, I always had a camera on me. For my eighth birthday, I had a Rollerblading party with my squad. To practice, I put on my skates, and of course my dad made sure to film the whole training session. The thought that there would be video evidence of any potential failures immediately put pressure on me. Some of us humans don't love pressure. We prefer a relaxed and supportive environment.

(Hey, schools everywhere, do you hear that? Stop testing the kids! Every kid is different! Hold on, I need to go meditate.)

As I was blading around a corner, partway through the practice session, I fell and instantly started crying to my dad. "This is your fault!" I shouted, snorting afterward. "You were filming me! I wouldn't have fallen if you wouldn't have filmed me!" Honestly, that might be true.

My dad, although sympathetic, couldn't help but laugh at me from behind the camera. He has a very loud, distinctive goose honk of a laugh that he's passed down to his adorable daughter. His loudly laughing at me might have been the moment when I wired the connection of being on camera to making people laugh, even if it meant getting embarrassed to do so. But it also wired failure to feeling a heightened state of embarrassment.

Speaking of being embarrassed… One of the most embarrassing moments of my life was in fourth grade. It was picture day. I was

wearing white tights and a green dress. Which was weird because I
NEVER wore dresses. They made me uncomfortable. They still kind
of do sometimes. To this day, I have to force myself to dress in my
feminine clothes. I think it might be because I have a fear of being *too
seen* or being seen as someone who cares about her appearance. My
MO since I was a young person has been to make sure I don't let
anyone see me sweat (maybe that's part of why falling on camera upset
me so much). That meant not being too vulnerable except to those I
allowed to *see* all of me. Dressing comfortably, in the way that I felt
best represented me, was how I did that—that meant some sort of Gap
T-shirt, jeans, and sneakers. For me to dress up for picture day was a
BIG deal.

So, there I was in my dress in Mr. Rome's class, sitting at one of
those little colored plastic chairs with the desk attached and a cubby
underneath. Let me preface this by saying that Mr. Rome was a really
cool guy and that I thoroughly enjoyed having him as a teacher for
both fourth grade and fifth. (And no, not because I couldn't pass
fourth grade. I got straight B's!) To paint a picture of him, he was this
long-haired guy with a ponytail who played the guitar on Fridays and
had us all sing Beatles songs.

It was ten minutes until recess, and I really freaking had to use the
restroom. It got to the point where I actually had to raise my hand,
which was another big deal for me as someone not very outspoken and
who didn't want too much attention. For me to raise my hand back
then meant it was *urgent*.

"Mr. Rome," I said quietly. "Can I use the bathroom?"

"No, Manon. Recess is in ten minutes. You can wait."

I absolutely cannot wait! And my bladder agreed that this man was
insane. Still, I decided to wait one minute.

One minute went by.

Pressure was building, so I raised my hand again. "May I go to the
bathroom now, please?"

"Manon, you'll be able to wait a few more minutes."

Fine. I'll show him, I thought.

In an act of rebellion and revenge, I peed. In the seat. And this kid named Alex Richardson heard something dripping on the floor and looked over at me with this look of horror and complete disbelief, as if he were saying, *"Holy crap! She's pissing herself!"* with his eyes.

"Are you okay?" Alex asked hesitantly. "What are you doing…"

I just kept on tinkling in silence—but kept looking at him in that slightly guilty way that dogs do when they doo-doo.

My bladder was empty and my need for revenge was satisfied. But then the embarrassment started settling in around the same time my damp legs started getting cold. It hit me: *I just peed in public and everybody saw…*

Then, for some twisted reason, Mr. Rome made the other kids clean up my piss with paper towels. That's abuse, right? I feel like that was abuse.

"Oh no! Okay, Manon, I'm so sorry!" Mr. Rome said as he came running over. He knelt down before me. "I'm so, so sorry! I should have let you go! I had no idea that you had to go that badly! You can go now!"

Well, thank you, but I don't have to go anymore…

But I went to the bathroom anyway and stared at myself in the mirror, judging myself, beating myself up for what I had done. *What just happened? What did I just do? I'm an idiot.* (I'd witnessed my dad call himself that a few times in his office, so I started using it. Dad, you're *not* an idiot. You're a smart, wonderful man whom I love very much.)

Of course, what was intended as an act of rebellion and claiming my control turned into a focal point for my peers to tease me about. From then on out, my friends regularly teased me about that awful day. I became known as the "Princess of Pee." Okay, they never called me that, but I wish they did. I feel like I should have at least gotten a cool nickname from that whole ordeal!

Having gone through that, having experienced such an embarrassing moment at the age of nine or ten, I felt like there wasn't much more I could do to embarrass myself. After that day, I would almost purposefully make a fool of myself every chance I got. I'd speak to strangers in a Kermit the frog voice in grocery stores or dance all twinkle toes ballerina style in public at the movie theater to make my friends laugh. And their laughter was like music in my ears.

Years and years later, I told my therapist about that day. "What an interesting turn of events that you'd be a comedian after getting made fun of when you were younger. Then, you didn't have control over people laughing at you. But now, you've made a living by seizing control over when people laugh at you. You still *want* people to laugh at you, but you get to control it."

My response to that was, "Holy crap!"

When I was around nine, I went up to Whistler, Canada. My parents and I would go there every Christmas to visit my family at this beautiful house near a ski resort that my uncle designed. Uncle Paul designs ski areas all over the world, which, judging by his lifestyle, is a surprisingly lucrative career with tons of travel. I know this because he likes to talk about it. He also loves to talk about his record-breaking bowel movements. Okay, that was one time… but I'll never forget it. Anyway, it got very loud at dinner. There was always wine involved. A lot of wine.

The first few days of being up in the snowy Whistler winter wonderland were pretty fun. By December 28, my uncle and his wife went to Sun Peaks, leaving the rest of us with the massive house to ourselves. Occasionally, my dad's best friend, Mike Carson, would come up with his family. This particular year, his friend and his kids were up there with us, so there were a bunch of us in the house.

My dad liked to stuff my Christmas stocking with silly little knickknacks like whoopee cushions, Play-Doh, and something called a fart cup—which they now call a Flarp cup, because I think "fart" is not

PC anymore? I'm annoyed. What a *Flarp* cup is, is this cup with putty in it, and when you push the putty down it makes breathtaking sounds... of flatulence.

So, I'm looking at this thing, thinking, *This is not a stocking stuffer... what is this? I wanted cold, hard cash!*

The funny thing is, I would get one of these fart cups every year and I never knew where they went after Christmas was over. Maybe he grabbed the same one and kept putting it in. At least, I hope so, because spending money on a fart cup once a year is absurd. *Stop doing it!* Usually, I would just set it aside. But during this trip, I used it for this talent show thing we all used to do for entertainment. If you have ever seen *Dan in Real Life* with Steve Carell, it's like that scene where the family members take turns putting on a show for their relatives. Except I was the only performer. I guess I was just TOO intimidating to follow.

At some point around this time, I'd heard this beautiful classical song by Johann Strauss called "The Blue Danube" and it was just stuck in my head for-freaking-ever. (Please bookmark this page, go listen to it, and then pick this chapter back up. I promise it will make this story better!) For the show I put on, I had someone play this song and I danced along to it with the fart cup behind my back, making sounds of flatulence with it to the beat. Everyone *HOWLED!* Like cartoon wolves! It was weird. Some of them even fell to the floor.

I think they got such a kick out of it because I was so serious about it and because I was so on rhythm. That might have been my first time performing and improvising for an audience. And it felt *so* incredible! My body buzzed with endorphins, making me feel like I was on cloud nine!

The next day, they wanted another dance performance from me to "The Blue Danube." *Nothing is going to top what I did last night,* I thought. Trying to figure out how to make what I did just as funny put so much pressure on me. I had no choice but to make an announcement. I stood tall and proud and announced, "Attention! Just so you all know... Tonight's fart show may not be that funny."

That sent them into fits of laughter and I had no idea why. I mean, I get it now. A nine-year-old standing in front of a room full of their family and friends to soberly announce the cancellation of a fart show is a little ridiculous. And that was something they never let me live down. I find families love telling the same stories over and over. At the end of the day, all we are left with is our memories. They are precious. So, make some good ones.

Those two nights up at Whistler solidified the thought in my mind that I liked—no, *adored*—performing for an audience. Following that trip, I tried to seek out moments and opportunities to perform and entertain in some way.

Not long after the Christmas in Whistler, I joined drill team—a more serious, intense version of cheerleading that involved a lot of dancing to drum beats. In fourth grade, we got all dressed up in uniform with our hair tied up in buns like little mouse ears, and we competed at Birmingham High School and won first place out of ten schools! The next year we competed at Magic Mountain, clad in blue camouflage. That time we won first place again! Oh, how I love to win. IF I CAN'T WIN, THEN I DON'T WANNA PLAY!

Fifth grade is when I started my four-year-long singing career before I got all discouraged. One time I mustered up the courage to sing Ace of Base's "The Sign" in front of the whole school for some sort of sick group performance. The entire time, I was shaking. The words didn't come out the way I wanted them to. I thought for sure that I sounded like a not-so-talented, animated chipmunk. How I got myself to get up on that stage and finish, I'll never know. *That* may actually be the reason I'm not a professional singer. Who knows! Too many choices. I'll blame my father. We love to blame our parents for everything, don't we? It's all their fault. But then again...

My dad bought me a guitar around the time I graduated high school. I taught myself how to play instead of going to class so I could entertain all the new friends I was making in college. As well as my boyfriend at the time, Matt. (The one who got away... because I told him to go. I said I'd come back when I was ready. Shortly after, he found his now wife. People don't just wait. Write that down somewhere.) I performed a song that I wrote for Matt at Tropicana Gardens, which was our dorm at the time. After the dorm's open mic night, a lot of people approached me and said that they loved it. All of that positive reinforcement got me thinking that I should really rethink a singing career. But I still had my dad's voice in my head saying, "*Eh, it's just okay. It's good. But not good enough...*" I'm not even sure anymore if he said those exact words, but that's what I heard through the lens of my insecurity. Can we go back in time for the clip, please?

Maybe that's the reason I like doing the "indie singer" impression in my skits and stand-up. I feel like I can do that well, but, again, that might only be because I'm mocking all of the indie singers with the intent of getting people to laugh at me. So maybe I'll keep my singing satirical unless you all convince me to do otherwise. I'll be waiting for those DMs...

I wouldn't be the person I am today if I hadn't had this exact childhood. The first years of our life are the most influential. What we do, hear, and say in those first seven to ten years really sets a course for the rest of our lives. Whether you had the most horrific time growing up or the most perfect (but who has that?), the way to transform the feelings around it is to shift your perception of it. So, instead of being pissed off my whole life about peeing in public like a beagle, I can look for what it might have given me. Life events, parents, friends—they all give us something. I wonder what your past gave you? What did it make you fear, or *love*?

2

My First Love

I HAD MY first sip of alcohol when I was sixteen years old at my house when my parents were gone. I was with my friend Sara, and it was her second time drinking. She was showing me the ropes! The choice was between vodka and wine, so we chose vodka. It's what the cool kids were doin'. I had my vodka in a glass at the ready. I took a swig and thought, *Eww, WTF?* I made the instinctual choice to run to the fridge to grab some orange juice as a chaser, because that shit was nasty AF.

As you can imagine, since I was a teenager drinking for the first time, it didn't take long at all for that warm feeling to start settling in. Suddenly, colors became brighter and my body felt lighter.

What is this magical feeling? Is this what alcohol is supposed to make me feel like? Where are my thoughts going? Buh-bye... I've arrived.

After swaying for a bit, I thought, *I need to call my boyfriend, immediately... he needs to know about this.*

Sara and I danced all night in the living room. As a teenager who, like the rest of her counterparts, was struggling to find herself in that moment of inebriated bliss, I finally felt like I was who I'd always wanted to be. I felt the way I remember feeling when I was young and without a care in the world.

The next weekend, I *had* to do it again, but this time to excess. I went to a party and ended up drinking so much that I stumbled into a bathroom, hugged the potty like it was Brad Pitt, and then... blacked out. There wasn't much of that night that I remembered. But what I did remember was that I had a blast! Then, the following weekend, I did it again. And then again. That went on every weekend for years. There was nothing that I looked forward to more than high school parties where Jell-O shots were involved. I would always have, like, five and then move on to beer. Oh, how I loved a nice cold beer. Me and my girls would get together at one of our houses and spend hours getting ready. Well, they would. I always took less than ten minutes to get dolled up as my dad set a timer for everything I did. I'd be in my room editing videos or watching TV, and he'd come in and ask if I wanted to go to a movie. Of course, I'd say yes. Because I loved going to the movies.

Then he would say, "Great, get in the car!"

Umm... now?

"Yes, it starts in ten minutes."

My mother and I would run around the house getting our things together like two maniacs while my dad would be waiting in the driveway, the car running, his fingers drumming on the steering wheel. I'm laughing so hard while writing this because now it seems ridiculous.

A little warning would have been nice, Dad!

Needless to say, I get ready very fast and am usually the one waiting. All of my boyfriends have been very pleased with that.

Alright, back to the shots!

Alcohol made me feel confident, funny, tall, beautiful. All of the things I couldn't feel on my own when sober. I could say the things I didn't feel comfortable saying without it. We all want to be liked, and alcohol made me believe that what I said didn't matter and rather that everyone adored me.

And... cut to me throwing up profusely in my prom date's car. The poor guy cleaned it up while I slept in his bed.

Gosh, I was so classy.

Yes, alcohol was one of my first loves, and I wasn't done with it, not by a long shot. Pun intended.

3

What Happened in Vegas

SURE, IF YOU'VE heard one Vegas story, you've probably heard them all. But this little snippet of my life isn't really a snippet at all, but rather a bona fide catastrophe that serves as a window into one of the biggest personal struggles of my young adult life.

First, some backstory.

Flashback to seventh grade. The scene: I was strolling through Mr. Bostrom's class and I saw this girl named Tara with a binder that had a photo of JC Chasez from NSYNC on it. It was at that moment that I knew she and I were a match made in heaven and I instantly fell in love with her.

I looked at her and I said, "JC is my favorite NSYNC member!"

She said, "No way!" And then we basically became best friends forever...

And, oh, what perfect timing! She and I were both new to Calabasas. I had just moved there from Sherman Oaks, which is really only a twenty-minute drive from Calabasas, but that might as well be a world away when you're, like, ten. I went from having such a good group of girlfriends to knowing no one, getting made fun of on the bus, getting lollipops thrown into my hair, and getting told that my arms were too hairy. So, essentially, my self-esteem plummeted from that year onward. It was like being on a roller coaster that just kept going down, down, down. But then Tara came along at Woodland Hills and I had a true friend to face the world with. If we are lucky, we all get at least one.

Flash forward years later. I was twenty-two years old. My love affair with "Bobby Booze" was still going strong, and there was no better place to flaunt it than good ol' Las Vegas. Tara and I drove to Vegas with her boyfriend and the guy I was dating at the time, Chris, who was thirteen years older than me (not that it matters; the age gap is just for context). Older men tend to have a better idea of what they want, and it seemed like a lot of what the ones I met wanted was me. And it was nice to feel wanted. Plus, Chris was hysterical and reminded me so much of Robin Williams.

When we finally got to Sin City, we were sooo excited! And we did what pretty much anyone who's twenty-one and up does when they're on vacation in an exciting new place: shots, shots, shots, shots, shots, shots! Pretty much immediately.

Now, I always needed to eat before I drank. Hell, I always need to eat in general. Because I'm definitely an eater. Always have been. My first drugs of choice other than validation and attention were food and sugar. As a kid, I would just binge, binge, binge, and run around like a psychopath. Moving that much maybe helped the *tiniest* bit against becoming overweight. But I naturally always had an athletic build, so the food never really physically showed up. Like, I looked like a bodybuilder when I was eight, and for some reason I had such defined arms despite never once lifting weights. I have my mom to thank for passing on those genes...

Thanks, Mom! You're hot!

Now that I think about it, being naturally toned and running around the way I did in my youth, I potentially could've been a great athlete. But I chose to be a comedian instead... wise choice.

Ba-dum-tsh.

Back to Vegas, baby!

So, the four of us were sucking down every ounce of booze in sight and had some snacks, but we didn't eat a well-rounded meal. I blame my upcoming blackout on that. Why didn't they want to eat?! Were they just that excited? Did they think we could just sustain ourselves all night on booze? Was the goal just to get drunk as quickly as possible and save money without a legitimate meal delaying alcohol absorption? Perhaps I should give Tara a call after I finish this chapter and ask…

Anyway, we drank. *I* drank too much, per usual. The next thing I knew, I was standing in front of this club XS, which had just opened. I was hitting on the bouncers, and Chris, acting like his con artist self, decided to lie about all of our names, because they were only taking people on the list, which we weren't on. He called us "Ernie and Opps," which I still don't think were on that damn list, but because he was SO confident with his delivery, he got us into the club.

FO FREE, YO!

Pretty much all I remember is being near the pool. Now, maybe I blacked out, or perhaps I was roofied—I may have been roofied, and if I was, this was my only time being roofied—but I went from clubbing to blacking out to waking up at 5:00 A.M.… in the hospital… in Las Vegas… with IVs in my arm. After the initial shock at the situation I'd found myself in had dissipated, I looked away from the tube coming out of my arm to Chris, who was sitting there with his face in his hands, so disappointed, so worried about me.

Excuse me, good sir, but where were you when I was trying to drink everyone in Vegas under the table? Ahem.

Waking up in a hospital with no recollection of how I got there? Let me tell you, that scared the shit out of me. I felt so indescribably awful. I hated that feeling of shame, like I was the worst and most irresponsible person on the planet. What was wrong with me? Right there in that room I declared, "I'm never, ever drinking again! That was mortifying!"

By noon, I had left the hospital. Back at the hotel, I told the gang, "Sorry I scared the shit out of you! Sorry I made you worry all night for me! I'm never going to drink again so we don't ever have to worry about it!" I promised them that.

Oh, by the way, like pretty much anyone who drinks and has uttered a declaration that they're permanently abstaining from alcohol after a crippling hangover, I had made that promise maybe a hundred times prior to that. But here's the thing: alcoholism is so insidious, so cunning, and so powerful that you can swear on everything that you'll never drink again, and then, hours later, once the hangover fades along with the regret, once you start feeling better, the forgetter comes in and the dis-ease changes your mind and tells you, "*Eh, that wasn't that bad… One more time won't kill ya.*" But for many of us, it just might.

Later that second day in Vegas, the four of us had a pool party to attend. And not long after arriving at the shindig, I was drinking again—not a *ton*… but *again*…

It was only a few hours prior that I had woken up in a hospital scared shitless. I had *just* promised my best friend and my boyfriend that I wouldn't drink. And there I was. Drinking. Again. What? *A vodka soda won't hurt anyone! But is it ever just one with me?*

Diseases of the mind are baffling like that. One minute, you're in control. The next, you've gone back on your word and are strolling along a destructive path once again with no regard for the hard lessons you've learned or the risks waiting for you at the end of addiction's road.

There's an important lesson that was easy for me to learn but hard for me to live by: you can't get drunk if you don't take the first drink.

What a concept!

4

The Best-Worst Night of My Life

A S A KID, filming, editing, and directing music videos was my jam. Not for, like, MTV or anything. It'd basically just be me getting my friends together and telling them, "Okay, so you're going to lip-sync to Avril Lavigne or JoJo in three different locations and then I'm gonna edit it together!" And boom! I was a budding director.

That actually turned into a business for one summer. I'd film music videos for girls who were having their bat mitzvahs, so they'd feel like pop stars instead of just having a plain old video montage of their family with some background music that Grandma had picked out. Doing that for them—helping them look like rock stars, even for ten minutes—warmed my heart because it really got them to come out of their shells, which is incredibly important for any child in a world that places SO much emphasis on pretending to be something you're not. Teens are so scared. If only I knew when I was a teen that everyone was in fear, maybe I would have had an easier time and been kinder to others and myself. OH WELL! Coulda woulda shoulda! If you're a teen reading this, then please be nice to others. It'll be worth it later!

Working with these thirteen-year-olds and getting them in front of the camera, helping them to have fun and just be themselves, that was the most rewarding part—not the money, honey.

My passion for making goofy and fun videos developed into a lifelong dream of wanting to become a director. So, after high school, I went to community college at Moorpark College and Santa Barbara City College, where I took media studies, TV production, editing, and acting. I made the Dean's List (the good one, not the "Arrest upon sight" one), and I was, like, *fine. Thank you! Now where's the camera? I'm ready to direct!* And after three years of that, I decided to transfer to film school. There I was, trying to learn about film, and these guys still wanted me to take, like, anthropology and Chicano studies.

I always had a really hard time paying attention in class, mainly because I was addicted to sugar on top of constantly zoning out, due in part to wasting sooo much energy just trying to fit in. And it was already hard enough absorbing any of the information and trying to focus. Wasting extra energy on classes that didn't even pertain to what I was paying to learn seemed pointless.

Then I had one of those *I can't do this anymore! I hate school!* moments. That moment happened during my first week of classes at Cal State Northridge's film school. After my last class that Friday, I called my father and proclaimed, "Dad, I wanna quit school and do improv!"

And he was like, "Great."

Then I dropped out. See ya, school! You can suck it! Actually, I have a dream of going back someday and actually learning a thing or two. The number of things that I don't know is abysmal. At least I know the word "abysmal." I learned it from watching Joey learn it on *Friends! Friends* was more than just my comedy school!

I knew exactly what I wanted to do but didn't know where to begin this new improv journey I had my sights set on. And as luck would have it, my dad happened to be sitting on the couch with our family friend Hal, whom I've known my whole life.

Dad and Hal were both, like, "Well, we met at Second City..."

That blew my mind, because I didn't know they'd ever done improv at all, let alone together. Since Second City had this significance in my dad's life and resulted in an amazing experience and a lifelong friendship, I ended up choosing that as where I'd start my comedy journey.

If you haven't heard of Second City, it's an improv group that started in Chicago; Tina Fey and Steve Carell, among so many others, started their careers there. It was at the ripe old age of twenty-one that I attended the one in Hollywood. That's where I met some of my really good friends, like my best friend in the world, Travis, as well as a couple of other amazing friends whom I'd later begin creating funny content with.

Oh, and the teachers at Second City… I loved them! You know you have a good comedy teacher when you want the talent they have and they truly make you laugh. One teacher pulled me aside once and told me, "In a row of cans, you're like the dented one." That confused me until she said, "You stick out."

That fed my ego! Thanks, Jamie.

I remember watching the masters at work, laughing hysterically while thinking, *Oh my God, they are hilarious! Let me soak up all the knowledge!*

Those comedy gurus imparted so many valuable lessons to us, nurtured our talent, had us playing games—it was all just so fun and fulfilling. Finding fulfillment there helped me realize my purpose. And I feel like my purpose on this planet is to play and essentially get back to the child that I was when I was… well, a child.

I feel like that's what so many people's journey is: getting back to that vulnerable state where they are present in the moment and they're not thinking about what they did yesterday or what they have to do tomorrow. And that's why I love improv so much. It's because I don't have to prepare anything. I just have to listen and respond. Talk about freedom!

At twenty-two years old, when I'd been studying at Second City for a year, my improv friends and I had a little post-class routine on Tuesday nights: we'd all go out to karaoke at Big Wangs in Hollywood. And I'd down either red wine or a Blue Moon before going on to sing my heart out. Now, "Mr. Jones" by Counting Crows was my go-to, but

I would sing Katy Perry's song "E.T." when I wanted to secretly confess my love to a specific someone in the bar. And during my performance, I would run around the place acting like I was in a music video the entire time. If you're going to sing, you have to commit and go full Super Bowl halftime show.

At the end of the night, after all the drinking and singing, I would either drive from Hollywood to Burbank to see my boyfriend Chris, or I'd head home to Calabasas, where I was living with my mommy.

On one Tuesday in particular, after karaoke, we all went to a place called Boardner's, which was this dark bar that had burlesque dancers performing on the back patio. Over the course of three hours, I had some nachos and around two and a half beers, which was nothing! It was a light night.

So, I thought to myself, *I'm good to drive!* Because, let's be real, roughly three beers is nothing! Especially when it's over the course of three hours. Like, it's pathetic for a night's worth of drinking.

Oh, I should also mention that, at the time, I was borrowing my mom's car because I had rear-ended someone in my Volvo and it was in the shop getting fixed. Fun fact: I had a habit of rear-ending people. Either I was texting, or I was totally unaware and just not present in my body at all. I've come to believe that the universe is trying to give us signs when things repeatedly happen, and if we don't get it, something bigger will happen to force us to make a change. For me, that big thing was about a fifteen-second drive from Boardner's.

All I did was pull out of my spot and roll on up to the light. That's when I noticed there was a cop behind me. Aaaand that's when the red and blue lights came on.

I was on my phone at the time, which is illegal, so, of course, my reaction was something along the lines of, "Ugh, now?!"

As the cop began his approach, I rolled down the window, then placed my hands on the steering wheel.

"Do you know why we pulled you over?" he asked.

And I responded with a very polite, "Because I'm cute?"

JK.

What I actually said was, "No, why? What's going on?" Because playing dumb usually works.

"Your lights weren't on…" he said.

The lights on my Volvo? They came on automatically. The ones in my mom's car did not. And I didn't know that. Which was *such* a dumb freaking reason to get pulled over.

Of course, when I tried explaining that I was used to driving a car with automatic lights and that this was my mother's vehicle, he smelled the beer on my breath.

"Have you been drinking tonight?" he asked.

While I do play dumb sometimes, I never lie. "Yes, but *not* enough to get me in trouble!"

"Okay, can you step out of the vehicle?" he said.

"Gladly," I responded. And then I did a little ballerina hop out of the car. Which, now that I think about it, probably didn't help my case.

Then he shined his flashlight in my eyes, which was *very* rude. He didn't do the backward-alphabet thing, which kind of sucks because I have half of it memorized. (Z, X, Y, W… then I always want to jump to P-U-T, which isn't at all accurate.)

The officer shut down my offer to recite the alphabet in reverse and instead had me walk in a straight line. And I did! I walked so straight! But then he still asked me to blow into the thingy (insert dirty joke here).

So, I blew into the Breathalyzer, thinking that if I were going to get busted for drinking and driving, it would have happened one of the many other times I may or may not have driven after drinking way more than I had that night.

And what did I end up blowing? A freaking *0.08…* which was the *exact* limit! Any other night, I would've blown a friggin' 2.0. And there were at least a hundred nights where I may or may not have been driving with a BAC that high! But I hadn't gotten caught. I was reckless. I was reckless because I thought I was invincible and nothing bad would ever happen to me because, you know, I thought I had a magical shield around me due to the fact that I just hadn't ever really gotten in trouble before.

So yeah, I only blew a 0.08, but guess what? They still decided to arrest me and take me in, which really upset me and ruined my night. The natural reaction to that was obviously to break down and sob my eyes out. FYI, I always cry. I love a good cry because I always feel so much lighter afterward. It's just an energy release, like laughing or flarping.

When I was all done, I was like, *Okay. I cried… it's done. Let's go have some fun!* With a nod, I rose from the curb and they put me in the back of the cop car. I asked if they were going to give me a ride back to my car. They were not. And this was before the days of Uber. I wish ride shares had been around back in those days! Woulda been real nice if they were!

Then we got to the station. And sitting on the bench was my friend from class Drew. He had gotten arrested as well! What a coincidence. The universe is so funny!

There we were, cuffed to the bench together, both of us gasping, "Oh my God!" at the sight of each other. Like two girls in high school who haven't seen each other since the day before.

Then I was like, "Drew?! What are you doing here, buddy!"

"What are you doing here, Manon?"

And we kind of giggled and started laughing, which definitely upset the officers.

Our brief moment of relief and joy from finding a familiar face in the pen was interrupted by this fierce-looking female cop who walked by and said, "This isn't speed dating," then proceeded to turn me around so we were back to back, because, for some reason, she didn't want us looking at each other. I think she was… having a bad night.

But what cop isn't? It has to be rough to be a cop. I mean, I think they have a great job, but I think it could be really hard.

Props to them! Thanks for all you do, cops! Much love.

If it were me, every time I'd stop someone, I'd be like, "You're fine. You're free to go!" But only if they were cute... hey, wait a minute...

I'd be the cop who let everyone off the hook. Unless they were doing something really bad, like trying to hurt someone or inflict harm on me. Then I would try to teach them a lesson, not by putting them in the slammer but by teaching them to love the parts of them that hurt so that they'd heal and not behave that way again. I probably wouldn't get accepted into the academy with that attitude. What a shame.

Back to the story... The cop finally approached me and said, "Okay, we have to take a mug shot."

Of course, I wasn't serious at all during that process. It was a whole lot of me being dumb and constantly posing for it Lindsay Lohan style. And then I asked the police if they were hiring... Because I was looking for a job. I was just being a smart-ass. Thankfully, at least one of the cops had a sense of humor and got a good laugh out of my antics.

"This girl's a comedian!" he said, grinning. "You're hilarious! You know, my son got arrested recently for drunk driving too!"

"Nice!" (I don't condone it and wouldn't dream of doing it again, but at the time, my disease was loud and overpowering any sense I had.)

It ended up being a really great night—you know, other than the part where I was alone for four hours in a drunk tank thinking that my life was over. That part wasn't great... and it's not great when you don't have any numbers memorized for your phone call. I mean, I did have one. It was my boyfriend's number, for some reason. Now, if I were to get arrested today, I don't know whose number I would know by heart. I think I'd end up calling my friend Danielle from when I was seven because I am incapable of ever forgetting that number.

When the four hours were up, they finally released me, and then I went to Chris's house and told him what had happened. The most mortifying part was confessing to my parents what had happened. That was THE most embarrassed I'd ever been. Because I had heard about people getting DUIs in my high school and it was always the *"really bad kids."* Again, I'd never been in trouble before, so for me to get arrested didn't make any sense and it was just a humiliating experience.

It was painful but humbling. It was also the best thing that's ever happened to me, because that night resulted in my stumbling onto a spiritual journey of self-discovery that changed my life forever.

5

The Guy Who Cried in a Strip Club

ONE WOULD THINK that the .08 experience, which landed me in a twelve-step program, would have been sobering (pun intended), but while the whole ordeal left me a bit shaken, all I could think after my first twelve-step meeting was, *That's cool. That's good for these drunks, getting the help they need. Good for those people!* Because, come on, I didn't need help! I was young! I didn't even have a problem! Binge-drinking and blacking out from time to time wasn't any different than what most kids in their early twenties were doing across the country. And having my license suspended? That wasn't the end of the world for me either. I was in the Los Angeles area, not the middle of rural West Virginia or something—getting around was not a problem. My whole take on my situation was, *Okay, I can't drive… This is the best! Now I really can drink!*

And then I did. A lot. For a while, too.

Then there was a point where I also didn't drink so much. And then I had a bit of a promiscuous month. A therapist once told me, "'Promiscuous' is just a shaming word for 'exploring sexuality.'" That made some shame dissipate.

As the holidays passed and 2012 approached, I told myself, *Okay! This is my resolution! I think I'm done. No more alcohol!* Suffering from stress-induced ulcerative colitis might have played more of a role in that resolution than being in the twelve-step program did. The funny thing is, I had been diagnosed with it at seventeen. Wait, did I mention that I started drinking at sixteen? The doctors had told me not to drink.

As you know by now, I didn't listen. When I heard that, I was like, *Cool… I'm definitely NOT going to stop drinking because this is ONE of the few joys of my life, so you can SHOVE IT, doc…*

Here's the thing about alcohol: For those who struggle to fit in, like me, and for those suffering from social anxiety, like I did, alcohol is like a medicine. When you take that medicine away—when you take away a person's social lubricant that they need to function comfortably— they're left with themselves, their symptoms, the pain of social pressure and expectations, and their thoughts. Let me tell ya, doing karaoke, dancing, and hanging out with friends where everyone was drinking and letting loose while I was sober was HARD. Especially after beer, wine, and liquor had been my crutches for years. Without those *meds*, I became so aware of my actions and I began to worry about how everyone was judging me (when they were all probably just living in the moment). Then it became a constant struggle to learn to be confident and comfortable in my own skin.

In my teens I envied my friend Codi for that reason. She was a musician, and somehow, she'd go to all the high school and college parties and she wouldn't drink—ever. And I admired how confident she seemed at parties without needing social lubricant to endure it all. She was my shining model for a sober person. Because I couldn't do that. The thought of deciding not to drink anymore just had me like, *Ugh, man, I can, like, dance on tables when I get shots in me. But if I'm not going to drink, I just won't go to the party…* Because the thought of being out in public sober? That was fucking boring.

But there was always this quiet thought in the back of my mind that was like, *At some point in my life, I want to be like Codi. I want to be able to be out and be me and shine and be confident without drinking to get myself there. Man, that would be a dream.* But it felt so far-fetched. So far away, so unrealistic.

But damn it, I tried. And at the time it felt difficult, considering this was after I had moved out of my mom's Calabasas apartment into a

Sherman Oaks house that was inhabited by three eighteen-year-old party girls who had *just* graduated freaking high school. *Thanks, Craigslist…*

Our environment strongly affects who we are, just as much as our genetic makeup can. To a degree, we become our surroundings, or at the very least we can be greatly influenced by them. Like Tony Robbins says, "proximity is power," and the five people you spend the most time around are what you're going to become. And there I was, spending all of my home life around a bunch of eighteen-year-old girls, one of whom was a dancer who got half-nakie onstage. I was five years older than them, drinking the amount they were drinking, and I was like, *Okay, something is wrong with this picture…*

Sure, it could've been a lot worse. They could've been meth heads or heroin addicts. Or murderers. But the timing sucked, because I was finally trying to better myself, yet I was burdened with negative influences.

One night, my stripper roommate, Tera, came into my room while I was drinking wine, watching my *friends* Phoebe and Ross do their thing. Could they *be* any funnier?

"I'm going to perform tomorrow night," Tera said cheerfully. "You should come watch!" I think it was at the Tiger Den or something like that in Studio City.

Because I'm a good human, I went to support her, along with our other roommate, Lauren. And Lauren? To paint a picture of her, imagine a bleach-blond, tattooed girl with piercings and crooked teeth who spoke with a Wisconsin accent. No lie, this girl had a different boy in her bedroom *every* night.

Lucky bitch…

As Lauren and I sat and watched Tera dance, I remember a reoccurring thought popping up in my head. *I could do that… I'd be a fantastic stripper.* I'd like to think that in another life, I could've been a star stripper. Name of my first novel: *The Star Stripper.*

Anyway, during the show, these three *very* good-looking guys strolled into the strip club. One was a hot long-haired actor whom some may recognize now. Another was this Cuban-Russian-Latin dude named Tony. There I was, drinking my usual vodka soda with lime— one in one hand, another ready to go in the other—and sitting across from Tony and his open button-down shirt. Tony and I got to talking and he was actually *present.* I'm talking attentive, listening, and responding to me while there were strippers working hard onstage to get his attention. We started talking about our journeys in the entertainment industry and how hard it could be. And then, out of nowhere, Tony's eyes began watering and he started crying in the strip club. As far as I know, he wasn't drunk. I think he may have had a drink, but I don't remember seeing him drink anything from the time he walked in.

Either way, I was stunned, not because he was crying but because there was something so very authentic about him. He wasn't trying to hide his emotions. Tony was so completely in his heart that I became enamored with him and kind of obsessed. But then, at the end of the night, I hooked up with… his roommate.

Ay, yi, yi.

It was either that night or the next that I found Tony on Facebook. I spent most of winter break talking to him online, trying to get him to go out with me. It wasn't just because of physical attraction. It was how genuine he was; it was the way he wore his heart on his sleeve that was attractive to me at that point. That was so alluring because I didn't know how to do that or be that way myself yet. And I'd never been with a guy who could do that. I had always just dated other alcoholics, and before that, I was in high school, where everyone was shy and covered up and not who they were yet. Of course, I played it cool with Tony and basically begged him to go out with me. I was used to boys falling in love with me in seconds, so begging was something I only did when I wanted another drink.

Here I was being all vulnerable and showing him how badly I wanted a date, and he had the nerve to reject me for some stupid reason! He had some lame-ass excuse like, "No, Manon… you hooked up with my roommate…"

"Okay, let's put that aside," I countered. "That's the past. You can't be mad at the past. Let's focus on our future." Then I kind of manipulated the situation by saying, "Let's just be friends then."

January finally rolled around. By this point, I had grown sick of my roommates. There was this one night when they all went out and I had the house to myself. I grabbed the ol' guitar and just started playing really loudly—you know, like Macaulay Culkin in Michael Jackson's "Black or White" video. Then an epiphany struck while I was jamming out.

Damn, this is amazing… Being home alone playing guitar in the house… I wish I could do this more often… Oh my gawd, I should live alone!

A few days later, my dad drove me around so I could find a new bachelorette pad. Not long after setting out, we drove to one place on Moorpark Street in Studio City that was absolutely a dream. The next thing I knew, I was moving into my very own Fortress of Solitude.

My apartment was within walking distance of my job at Daily Grill, which was awesome because I still couldn't drive because of my .08 fiasco. It was also on the same street as the twelve-step meetings that I would later go on to attend every day at 3:00 P.M. I also found an Irish healer that I still go to every once in a while on Moorpark Street. At the time, she was a healer of thirty-five years. Her first client was a dreamy A-list celebrity. Since then she's pretty much worked on all the who's who, including little ol' me! Also on Moorpark was M Street Coffee, the place where I eventually did my fourth step (making a moral inventory of yourself). It goes without saying that this vortex of a street essentially became my power street and changed the trajectory of my life.

Eventually, Tony took me up on my offer to just be friends, so I
went ahead and invited him to my new apartment to have a friendly
chat. He sat on one couch, I sat on the other, and we talked for five
hours. Then, just like he had on the night we'd met, he started crying.
Like, how can someone be so in their heart that they cry that much? I
could've been confused and I could've gotten freaked out and walked
away. But, again, I had never seen that kind of vulnerability in a guy my
age. And at that time in my life, I was just craving anything authentic,
anything real.

I was two weeks into the new year and had managed to remain
sober. Resolution complete. With half a month of sobriety under my
belt, it no longer seemed so impossible to keep it going. And at this
point, I definitely wanted to keep it going. So, when my friends wanted
to head out on the town one night, I joined them with the intention of
exercising my newfound self-control.

Tony joined us on our night out. Of course, all of my friends
drank—not that I didn't expect them to. Even Tony had some
champagne that night. It didn't take long for that little voice in my head
to go, *Eh, fuck it.* As it turned out, I hadn't really developed a mental
defense against that first-drink temptation. Because the next thing I
knew, the flute glass was to my mouth and I was sucking down some
of that bubbly champagne.

In no time, I was drunk-dancing with my friends, bouncing around
like a coked-up lemur. For some reason, Tony didn't want to dance, so
he just sat there sulking on the couch, which kind of pissed me off. So,
I said, "Screw this," and kept dancing and dancing without him, until I
decided to go back over to where he was sitting to see if I could get
him to change his mind.

It was immediately clear from his expression that he was upset with
me. "Manon, I'm going to go… I'm going to get a cab… I'm going
home," he said.

"What? Why are you leaving?" I asked.

"Because you're being disrespectful. You're out there dancing with other guys right in front of me… Why did you even invite me here?"

Okay, in hindsight, I see now that he was being incredibly insecure. I mean, we hadn't even freakin' *kissed* yet! In my mind, I'm thinking, *Grow some balls, dude! And if you want to dance with me, then fucking take me and dance with me! DIP ME, damn it!* That's what I should have vocalized at the time.

"Oh my God! I'm so sorry, Tony!" is what came out instead. Because I didn't want to lose him. (Come on, we all have our moments of desperation.)

He and I spent the rest of that night arguing. It got to the point where my friend's brother came up to me and asked, "How long have you been dating?"

I snorted. A laugh followed. "Dating? Oh, we haven't even kissed yet…"

This was my third time hanging out with Tony and we were already fighting like an old bickering couple, and the whole experience was absolutely mortifying to me.

Eventually, he just straight-up told me, "No, I'm not into you. That behavior is not attractive to me, so I'm leaving." Not to sound vain or anything, but this was the first time a guy had ever really rejected me. Well, first he'd rejected me on Facebook, and now he was rejecting me again.

"You will not reject me!" I declared, trying to use my Jedi mind-trick powers to bring him back in. But nothing was working! None of my tactics were effective.

Oh my God, what am I going to do? I can't be rejected, I thought. I had gone from never begging to begging for the second time in a month, one final act of desperation to get this guy to stay. And he did.

Tony and I spent most of the night talking and making up. Being outright rejected by him due to drunk Manon's behavior and hearing what he had to say must have triggered something deep in me, because (spoiler alert) that was the last night that I consumed a drop of alcohol. Of course, I didn't know it would be at the time.

Soon after that night, Tony and I got serious. Most of the people in my life are very funny, which makes me feel really blessed, because I can't state enough just how healing laughter is. I don't think I would've been able to get through what I got through had I not kind of been laughing through it. That being said, everyone I've ever dated has had a really, really good sense of humor, too. Except for Tony. He HAD a sense of humor. It just didn't align with MINE.

One time he actually told me, "I've just never found women to be funny." And yes, he was very serious. Like, he firmly believed it.

Why am I dating this person? You're saying this to the wrong person...

But then I dated him for six more months. As if that weren't enough of a red flag that I was with the wrong person, after I kissed him one time, he backed away and said, "Sometimes I'm just afraid you're a porn star."

I leaned back, brows raised, eyes blinking rapidly. "Um, whaaaaat? I'm your girlfriend... We've been together for how long now? You *know* I'm not a porn star." Though that was random as hell and so very weird, I didn't take it personally. (For the record, I'm STILL exploring my sexuality and have a lot more to learn. I'm nowhere near as confident as porn stars. Remember, I can barely wear a dress.)

The fact that I kept dating him even after he said those two things baffles me. His major jealousy issues, on top of his being wildly insecure, should have been enough for me to break it off. Whenever I was at his place, he basically forbade me to talk to his roommate. Acting like someone doesn't exist is not what I am about. I want to be a friendly, open person to all people. But I wasn't true to myself then. I catered to Tony's insecurities rather than challenging them by saying, "Well, no, I'm a friendly person. I'm going to say hi to your roommate because I'm in their house. Love is abundant, so why can't we all just connect?"

Catering to his insecurities ended up being a detriment to me, because I started feeling like I was shrinking and not being who I really was, all to feed *his* ego and make *him* feel comfortable. And making yourself smaller to be with someone else? That will never work! It will always lead to resentment, because our souls want to be expansive. Any time we're not being who we really are for someone else, the relationship is destined to crash and burn. And I believe that's where many diseases and health problems come from. Not always, of course. There are many people in the world with health conditions that a happy affirmation can't fix. And my hat goes off to anyone who is dealing with a true mental health disorder, because that takes a lot of courage and soul searching that other people don't have to deal with. But if I didn't have inflammatory bowel disease or alcoholism, I wouldn't have written this book. SO BOOYA! So much good can come from the hardest things in life.

So I eventually ended it with Tony because I knew there had to be more out there for me when it comes to love. I had to have a relationship with someone who thought women were funny. You know, because I'm a frigging comedian. I needed another change. And it was coming in fast.

6

Something *BIGGER* Than Me

L ITTLE DID I know when I woke up on Monday, January 30, 2012, that I'd be changing the trajectory of my life. It surely didn't feel like it; it seemed like the start of just another week to me.

My schedule looked a little something like this: Monday through Friday I worked from 10:00 A.M. until 2:00 P.M.—long hours, I know. I *slaved* away at the Daily Grill as a *servant girl*. I started in the takeout area. Takeout was toward the bottom of the totem in the hierarchy of employees. Management felt sorry for us common folk, so they let us take commission from food orders, which was SICK because the Italian restaurant that I worked at before Daily Grill didn't do that. I had it MADE. Daily Grill was across from CBS studios, so we'd get a lot of the *Mindy Project* and *Arrested Development* traffic, which I actually made pretty good money from—enough to afford to live in that Studio City apartment that felt like a damn palace to me. Eight hundred square feet of HEAVEN. To have my own space? Are you kidding me? Yes, please; more, thank you! I think everyone should have a chance to live alone if they can. It's one of the best, most liberating feelings.

After my work shift on that life-changing Monday, I walked on over to a 3:00 P.M. twelve-step meeting, still not convinced that I was an alcoholic. Ya know… because I wasn't homeless or on skid row.

At that meeting I remember feeling a sensation in my hand that made it shoot up. I had the thought, *What am I doing! I don't want to look like a fool but I also can't help that my spirit apparently needs to be heard.* I got called on, and the words that came out of my quivering mouth were, "Hi, my name is Manon and I'm an alcoholic." Cue sobbing.

First, please know, I didn't say it because I actually thought I was; I did it so I could fit in at the meeting. Everyone was there sharing and trying to heal, and there I was in spectator mode acting like I was in detention for something I hadn't done. But then, unexpectedly, saying out loud that I had a problem with alcohol forced me to see myself in a new way. A softer, more loving way. The tears started streaming from my eyes and they haven't really stopped since. Well, that's not true, but I do cry a lot. And I don't intend to stop!

Here's a rough transcript of the thoughts that ran through my head when those words left my mouth: *Wait... Am I an alcoholic? Oh my God... Is that what it is? Oh my God... IS THAT WHAT IT HAS BEEN THIS WHOLE TIME? Is that why I'm living my life the way I am? Is that why I drink so much? I guess it is kind of a problem that I black out almost every damn time I drink.... Am I bodily and mentally different from my fellows?!*

The twelve-step program is about attraction, not promotion. I don't know about you, but I don't like being sold to. When someone says I "should" do something, I want to vomit and run the other way. But when I see someone who looks like they have it together and what they're doing is bettering their life, they are effortlessly attractive; I walk right toward them without knowing why sometimes. That's the difference between being promotional and being attractive. And I was very attracted to the kind of energy that was going on in that meeting there that day, for some reason. That genuine, authentic quality that had moved me in Tony was the same kind of truth I experienced in the meeting on that day.

Suddenly, I realized the insane extent to which I dearly loved alcohol—I realized that my entire life was revolving around when, where, and with whom I would consume it. It truly was like one of those Lifetime movies where a woman is so enthralled by a relationship when it's obvious to everyone but her that it's completely toxic.

Now that I'd had yet another good cry, I was feeling lighter. *Yeah…
I think I need to change…*

Finally acknowledging that I had a problem, deciding that I had to
get my life in check there at that moment—that's when the healing
process started taking place for me. We can't change if we don't know
what's wrong! And, no lie, from that day on, everything in my life
started to get better, and really quickly. It wasn't even months later that
I ended up quitting my job at the Daily Grill, then randomly blew up
on Vine and got millions of followers. I mean, there's a bit in between
that I need to cover, but just for some context, that's how rapidly my
life improved. To be clear, my life got brighter because the fog of my
screwed-up perception of life had lifted and I was able to witness
beauty rather than dwelling in my sorrows.

'Tis the power of self-improvement.

Now that I was super serious about my sobriety, I began my first
week of the process by getting a sponsor. I had a lot of women from
the program ask if they could call me. *Call me? WTF? Why do these ladies
want my number? This is creepy.* At first it sounded strange to me, but I
quickly learned that's how it works. Spreading the message of hope to
another who is suffering is basically like taking a drug. After my first
week of sobriety, I sat through a meeting for younger newcomers to
the program, and this cool, hip chick named Ella started chatting me
up. I assumed she wanted to call me like everyone else, but then she
said, "I'm not going to call you. If you're serious about this, you can
call me." Whoa! She was badass. I liked the challenge, so I called her
the next day. Then, boom, I had a sponsor.

Not long after, Ella and I met up at a Chipotle and she got to
sharing her story with me. She was a down-to-earth astrologer with an
awesome mullet, and on top of that she was vegan (which blew my
mind at the time because my diet consisted of bacon, booze, and
bacon). We ate burritos together and she shared her vulnerability with
me. Her story was nothing like mine, but the feelings we had were the

same. That is what made me feel connected to her—to all alcoholics, really. The details don't matter as much as the feelings inside that we share. The pain, the fear. We all have it in some form or another and it's IN OUR WAY. Be gone, fear. BE GONE!

Me and Ella would meet up regularly at coffee shops and she'd read the recovery book with me. And in the program, they suggest we come up with a higher power of our own understanding. Because apparently, I wasn't God? That was news to me! I didn't know how to find a power greater than *moi*... I mean, I've always kind of been a spiritual person but I didn't really understand what spirituality meant to me; I didn't come from a religious background. To put things in perspective, I went to church maybe five times in my entire life. And I guess we'd pray before dinner, reciting the ol', "God is gracious, God is good. We thank you for this food, amen." But even then, I didn't know what I was praying to. It was a fun ritual but I had no concept of this so-called God that people were referring to.

So, that's what I told Ella.

"That's actually very common," she said to me. "So, what's cool is, you get to come up with your own conception of a higher power. Anything that's bigger than you!"

"There's a power greater than me? Uh, I don't think so..." I joked. Because at this point, as far as I knew, I'd been the one running the show of my life. And I hadn't been doing the best job. Being in charge of my life, making sure life went okay, making sure everything went right? That was A LOT of pressure on me. It was no wonder I drank.

"Well, Manon, there's a power bigger than you that's working in your life—hence the alcohol-induced arrest, maybe?"

And I went, "Wait a minute, whaaaaa?"

"It led you here, didn't it?"

"Yeah. And I feel really good right now. So that's true, I guess..."

"Well, think about this. Has your heart been beating for twenty-three years?"

"Yes…"

"Okay. And do you sit there and go, *Beat now. Beat now.* Or does it do it whether you like it or not?"

"I guess it does it whether I like it or not…" I said skeptically.

"Yeah, because there's a power greater than you making it beat. What if I told you to go to the beach and stand before the ocean and tell it to stop moving?"

I laughed. And then I realized, *It's going to keep moving because the ocean is much more powerful than I am… oddly enough.*

Answering those questions turned out to be all I needed to convince me that a power greater than me exists. I choose to call this power God for no other reason than because I like the word. I also adore the word "love." God is interchangeable with love. Love and God are the same to me.

Then Ella suggested that I incorporate prayer into my life as a way to realign my thoughts with more loving energy. I could also give my issues over to this God energy thingy. Now I had this power that was capable of solving all my problems and loved me unconditionally, which was an unexpected relief. It almost felt too easy, like slipping into a warm bath. Unconditional love from something outside of myself was therapeutic, because I realized that I had so many conditions in place for me to love myself, and I always fell short of those conditions and ended up hating myself, which often led to me self-sabotaging so that I wouldn't fail to meet those very conditions that I myself had established. Because if I failed, I wouldn't like myself. I relied on liquid courage because it made me feel like a QUEEN. Then I'd sober up and realize, *Nope, that was just the alcohol, it's a lie.* I'd spend the whole next day feeling so emotional, sick, and over life. *Okay, great… time to get drunk again so I can get that courage and confidence back.*

So, after many vain attempts at trying to quit alcohol, it was not until I finally admitted that I had an issue that I realized there was something in my life that needed correcting. I didn't drink every day, I didn't do heroin, so I'd thought that, clearly, I didn't have a problem. Before I went to meetings, I thought I wouldn't belong because it would just be a bunch of old men with brown paper bags who drank themselves into ruin daily. But in truth I saw hot, young people peppered in with celebrities. *I DO BELONG!* There were other girls like me who didn't drink alcohol in the mornings. And because I did what I was told to do and looked for the similarities between myself and others when I went into the meetings, not the differences, I was able to feel connected to the people there and actually hear the powerful messages being shared.

It was then that I was able to discover what spirituality meant to me, which allowed me to develop a sacred source. Mel Robbins says "the opposite of addiction is connection," and I believe that to be true. I get so much love and connection now that having a drink seems so much less appealing.

I went to the meetings often because I had been drinking often. Eventually, one week of sobriety turned into four and I got my thirty-day chip. To celebrate, I jumped off a bridge! With a bungee cord attached to me. I went with some other sober women to the Bridge to Nowhere. It was a beautiful five-mile hike up to the bridge, which felt like it took forever to reach. And let me tell ya, jumping from that high up was one of the scariest things I've ever done. But getting sober was scarier.

In order to jump, your want has to be bigger than your fear. And that really shows you how powerful fear is. Because if we're too afraid to do something, that fear is what holds us back. So my desire to jump had to be strong. And my *TRUST* that I was not going to plummet to my doom had to be equally strong. It's kind of symbolic. Like with the higher power, I had to trust that the bungee cord would not break. The quality-controlled manufacturing of that cord was something bigger than me. The fact that the people in charge of the event told me that no one had ever died from doing this meant statistically there was something bigger than me in play that would keep me from hitting rock bottom.

When I jumped and began falling forward, I just remember feeling every emotion. I cried, laughed, screamed, got angry, giggled. And that hike back after was just pure euphoria! I had just hit my thirtieth day of being sober and bungee-jumped off of that bridge. Let me tell ya, that was one of the happiest days in my entire life. The endorphins were flowing!

Life felt simple during this time. I really didn't mind my job at Daily Grill. I was with Tony and he didn't drink much, which made staying sober a lot easier for me. I had great friends. My body was healthier. It was an amazing beginning to my sobriety when I look back.

Even now, it's all still so strange to me because I lived a lot of my life burdened by alcohol addiction. Okay, I only really drank from sixteen to twenty-three, so I didn't have a long drinking career, but it just felt very full, and enough happened in those years to make it seem like a lifetime.

It's crazy to think that I went from living with three eighteen-year-old girls, drinking my head off, to living alone and becoming sober for the long haul in a matter of months. And it blows my mind that the positive changes didn't stop there.

7

#Impression

THE CURTAIN WAS closing on my two-year stint at Second City not long after I began the whole sobriety-and-spirituality thing. At this point, I was in the conservatory program, which ended with our performing an eight-week running show called *Friends with Medical Benefits*. Drew, the guy I'd seen down at the precinct the night I got arrested, and my other friend Amy, who later became one of my comedic partners, were both in it. Let me tell ya, that show was really, really fun. Of course, *I* thought it was good and that I was *sooo* funny back then. Now, looking back, I think, *Wow, I was really in my head a lot during our performances and I was actually pretty damn quiet onstage.*

That could explain why my theater teachers were always like, "Manon, you need to *PRO-JECT*! We cannot hear you!"

There was obviously a reason that I was quiet. Of course, that reason was fear. I was scared that if I said the wrong things, I would have to face rejection. Not that the teachers ever gave me a reason to be averse to stepping out of my comfort zone and performing confidently. They would always provide me with positive reinforcement, saying things like, "What you're saying is so funny and we're missing it…"

I heard their encouragement but I never followed their advice, so quiet I remained. That's part of the reason I've come to like stand-up— because you can use a microphone, so I can still kind of speak in a soft voice.

There was a point toward the end of my Second City days where I just started feeling so drained. I'd gone from working takeout at Daily Grill to being promoted to waitress, and servicing tables all day was using a lot of my energy before classes. One day, this thought just popped up in my head: *If I keep giving my attention to being a waitress, then I'm not giving it to my creativity. And if I'm just split between comedy and work, then I won't have any energy left for other things. So I think I have to release myself from this job.*

The idea of quitting was terrifying as hell, because I really didn't have any money saved. I'm blessed with supportive parents, so I knew that if my financial situation got really bad, I wouldn't end up on the street. But I didn't want to have to rely on my parents, and no matter your circumstances, it's scary to give up the predictability and simplicity of a stable job to dedicate yourself to a creative life that might not pay the bills. Nevertheless, I took the proverbial leap. Just like when I jumped off the Bridge to Nowhere, I had faith that something bigger than me would catch me before I hit rock bottom.

I remember putting my two weeks' notice in and feeling really good. At the end of two weeks, I celebrated my newfound freedom by venturing to New York with my friend Danielle. Going to watch clown shows was a part of our itinerary. And later, I actually signed up for clown school. Fun Manon fact: I did a ton of clown school. Come on, how else was I supposed to be a well-rounded comedian?

My friend Amy, who's a little younger than me, was going through her own spiritual journey around that time. She basically lived in a dungeon, so since we were good friends, and since I felt like I was her mentor/life guide, I said, "You need to come live with me! I'll take you in like a stray cat! Just don't scratch the furniture. And please don't pee on my rug." *You know how I feel about pee!*

She took me up on the offer, and I was back to having a roommate. At least she was much, much better than those three *wonderful* (cough, cough) girls that I'd lived with before.

This random app called Vine was generating buzz at this point, so, as lovers of all things that produce laughs, Amy and I hopped on it. The Vine app consisted of six-second videos that looped, and people were using it to create funny videos. I should mention that I was five months sober and, you know, all *spiritual,* so I didn't have any social media because I needed to connect and be present in the world at all times. *Let me make it so no one will be able to find me or contact me while I'm living life,* was the mentality that I adopted to avoid distractions. Yet, I caved… Why, you might ask. Because, Vine and comedy? They pretty much went hand in hand. And comedy is life.

Symptoms of Vine exposure manifested in us the way they did in everyone. It started with our watching Vine videos a few minutes a day, doing a lot of laughing out loud. Then it was a few hours a day, as we sent each other funny videos when, half the time, we were in the same room. That's about the time I started dating a celebrity (which I'll get to later), and then Amy and I went to do a little film in Big Bear for a week. When we came back, we realized, *Wait… we're comedians… We can totally make funny Vines!*

So, we did. And we were having so much fun goofing around creating content just for shits and giggles. At this point, having a following wasn't in the realm of possibility. Nor was it a goal, really. Becoming a director was the dream I was working toward. I loved improvising, but I thought, *Well, if I take acting classes, maybe I can become an actor, and then I can become a director sooner than if I just tried to make it as a director.*

I had also started taking a stand-up comedy class. It was a random recommendation from a coworker at Daily Grill. One day at work, she looked at me and said, "You know, you kind of look like Kristen Stewart."

Out of nowhere, I did an impression of Kristen Stewart right there on the spot, and not to brag, but this woman laughed really freaking hard, which made me very happy.

When she finally calmed down, she fanned herself and said, "You should take classes at Pretty, Funny Women." Then she told me all about the stand-up comedy school and how it helps create a safe environment for women to work out their jokes and get onstage.

"I should take classes there!" I cheered.

Not long after we started creating on Vine, I did my first stand-up show at Flappers Comedy Club in Burbank. It was a five-minute set where I came up onstage dancing, because I can't help but dance when I hear music. Music is in dis blood! After I caught my breath, I grabbed the microphone, told a few jokes, and did an impression of Kristen Stewart getting therapy from Kim Kardashian. Just BRILLIANT, I say! The audience lost it, which was the most amazing feeling.

That first stand-up performance was one of the best nights of my life. My dad came to the show and he later revealed that he retreated to the bathroom after my set and started crying. He wept tears of joy because I was living out his dream and he was just so gosh-darn proud of me. And my dad is not a crier, so that meant a lot to me. Weeks before I had told him that I was going to get onstage and tell jokes, and he'd looked at me with concern and basically said, "No way." Ya know, in that moment I had a choice: I could listen to his fear or listen to my risk-taking GUT. I'm happy I trusted myself in that moment. I know he was just trying to protect me. Proved ya wrong, eh, Pop?! Now he comes to every single one of my shows. Unless it's outta state, dawg. I think he would be a great stand-up. So whenever you're ready, Dad, I'm right here to support YOU. Just tell me when.

Since my first show got a lot of laughs, it led to doing a few gigs around town. I didn't do many open mics. They were long and boring and nobody really spoke to each other. Not only did they last hours, but they would go late into the night, and my bedtime is ten thirty! I value my sleep, people! I wonder whether I'd have a Netflix special by now if I'd really given it my all and showed up to open mics every night like many dedicated comedians. Oh well; I chose to focus on making short videos on my phone instead. I don't regret it.

One day, while Amy was out on some epic hiking trip up north, I was home alone making Vines for those amazing two hundred followers of mine.

Someone who had been at my comedy show the week before commented on one of the vids I posted, saying, "Throw up your Kristen Stewart impression! I saw you do it at the Comedy Store. It was so damn funny!"

That's a great idea!

So, I quickly put on that blue fedora that I had lying around, held my phone up to my face selfie-style, and said, "Hey, Kristen Stewart! What's your favorite ice-cream flavor?"

I ditched the hat (the Vine technique denoting a character change), then, as Kristen Stewart, I put a hand on my head, grabbed a fistful of hair, and with some dramatic, *Twilight*-inspired breathing mixed in, I went, "Um, um, I don't know…" I then added "#Impression" and "#KristenStewart" and posted it. I don't even remember how I knew I needed to do that… It was 2013 and I hadn't been on social media for a while, so I didn't even know what a hashtag was for at that time. But *THANK GOD* I added them!

After posting my last Vine of the day, I went out on the town for sushi with an ex-boyfriend for some reason that I can't even recall. That may have actually been our last meal together. He's happily married now, and I'm happy he's happy. I want all of my past loves to find true joy and peace in their lives.

So my booty hadn't even had the chance to warm up my seat in the restaurant when I started getting all of these notifications. Usually, I tried to be present over a meal with a human, but my phone never blew up like that, so the curiosity drove me to check. I looked down and saw that five hundred people had liked the Kristen Stewart video. Then there were a thousand likes for the video.

By the end of that night I had five thousand followers. And the next morning, I woke up to ten thousand followers! Almost as if it was a reflex, I just started jumping around like a little kid. "Are you kidding me right now?" I blurted out to no one, watching as the number kept going up.

From that day on, I kept making Vines every single day. And within a week, I had a hundred thousand followers. Within a month, I had a million... And then that journey definitely took off.

I couldn't believe what was happening. It was like being strapped inside a rocket! I was about a year sober, I had turned my will and my life over to the care of this higher power, and suddenly, things started opening up and messages started coming through. Amazing things were manifesting in my life, all because I chose to undergo a healing process through which I was able to get in line with my primary purpose. And my purpose was clear: be sober, be of service—and one of my services is to be creative and bring joy, laughter, and connection to as many people as I can. And I vow to do that until the day I die! BOOYA!

8

The Vine-Famous Life

L ET ME TELL YOU what one of the weirdest feelings of all time is: It's going from walking through the world relatively unnoticed to suddenly being recognized by strangers. Often. Daily. When it first started happening, it was surreal as hell but also pretty cool, in a way. And, weirdly enough, it somehow felt very natural. Familiar. Like, I didn't feel like I was famous or anything, I felt like I was just bumping into old acquaintances whose names I couldn't remember after years of not having seen them. I think that's how it could be for everyone though.

My dad used to say something like, "Strangers are the people you're dancing on the planet with at this time, so be loving and kind." Those words have stuck with me. They're a beautiful reminder that we are all truly connected.

Even before I became a public figure, whenever I saw people moving about in the world outside of my tiny bubble of existence, I didn't think of it as, *Oh, I'm me and they're them. Us* and *we* are always how I grouped myself in relation to strangers, friends, and family alike. In a way, my dad's message was similar to the lesson I learned in the twelve-step program—*look for the similarities in others, not the differences.* Obviously, no two people are exactly the same, but we share a hell of a lot more in common with each other than it seems if we look past the small number of differences. We're all here living, laughing, crying, trying to fit in, pursuing happiness, grieving, coexisting. So, when people who recognized me from their phones approached me, I took every encounter as an opportunity to connect, acknowledge, and embrace—that meant warm greetings and smiles for everyone. And hugs and photos for whoever wanted them! You know, because you can't just go around hugging everyone without their permission no matter how badly you'd like to spread the love. I mean, you can, if you have a hankering to get arrested.

From the time I reached influencer status until now, I've never had a poor encounter with anyone. Okay… actually, I can think of one time where someone seemed unenthused after meeting me. It was at Universal CityWalk. This group of teen girls around eighteen years old came up all smiley, then started barking demands like I was a monkey trained to dance on command.

"Can you do your Kristen Stewart impression?" they begged.

So I did. And they did *not* seem impressed with it. At all. They basically just turned and walked away when I was done.

Talk about awkward… Actually, I don't want to talk about it.

(Side note: I remember this model kissed me on the mouth one time, and she blamed it on my being awkward. Awkward is in the eye of the beholder. 'Twas a nice kiss though. I'd do it again. She's gorgeous. If you're reading this, come find me. I'll be the one in the corner of the place where we met, the one with the red rose.)

That single outlier of an experience aside, usually when people recognize me or meet me, they have smiles on their faces. That kind of response warms my heart so much, because it means I've been succeeding at providing the service of bringing joy and laughter to them the way I intended to.

For a while, Vining was just me uploading content daily, either by myself or with Amy. I dragged my best friend Travis into the world of Vine with me as well. Really anyone I could find. We frolicked to extraordinary places like Target, where we'd go down the aisles and film six-second, looping "masterpieces" with props gathered while browsing. One time I put on a hat and shades and did my best impression of Walter White from *Breaking Bad*. Of course, that meant that Travis played Jesse Pinkman. Goofing around in public, cracking up at each other's antics—it felt like we were teenagers all over again. Oftentimes we would spend hours in there making ten videos at a time. And that's why I loved Vine as a platform. There was no need to be profound, no need to be glamorous. You just did whatever silly thing came to mind and you were rewarded for it if it made people laugh. There was just no pressure at all, because it was just six seconds of material you could post on the spot, as much as you wanted, without any real algorithm to be a slave to.

For me personally, Vine was always about having fun in the moment. All of my videos were pretty much off-the-cuff. It was always spur-of-the-moment improv, like I learned from Second City. When we were coming up with skits on the fly, that's when things felt the most honest. In my opinion, I feel like when things were rehearsed, there was some crucial authenticity that got lost. Or maybe the energy flowed away.

The instant gratification of seeing people enjoying my content and reading all of the positive comments was definitely something I appreciated. It gave me that dopamine hit! To have anyone watching my content was kind of amazing, really. Like, hundreds of thousands of people witnessing me goof around seemed like such an insane concept. But I was so grateful that they were enjoying the spectacle that is Manon. It was good knowing that many people were laughing along with me (probably mainly at me). And the live feedback in the form of re-Vines, likes, and comments were all teachable pieces of information that helped me with my comedy, because I got to learn what bits worked best and which ones didn't.

The first time I ever got recognized, I was in Aroma Café in Studio City. This random guy just came up to me and said, "Hey, you're the Kristen Stewart girl! I follow you on Vine!"

I just laughed. "Hi! Oh my God! That's so funny! Yes! I am!"

"I have the same number of followers as you." He then proceeded to show me his account on his phone. "You know what? We should collab."

Smiling, I blinked rapidly. "Yeah! What's collab?"

It was clear by his face that he couldn't tell whether or not I was joking. "It means we would make a video together... " he said unsurely, squinting as he tried to read me.

"Oh. Okay... Why... ?"

"So we could cross-promote... And because a collaborative skit would be hilarious, freak." He laughed.

"Oh, okay, great... " I said, smiling, still very confused. The idea of collaborating on a social media app wasn't exactly something I'd experienced yet.

"Cool. How about you come over to my friend's house and we'll do some filming." He proceeded to message me an address.

Not gonna lie, venturing over to a random house to work with some stranger I'd randomly met had me a little sketched out. But he seemed like a really cool dude, and as I've learned, good things come when you step out of your comfort zone. So, I decided to go to the meetup.

At this first collab session, there were very well-known Viners. Getting to meet some of the creatives whom I admired for producing the content that had been making me laugh since I joined Vine, connecting with other Viners I hadn't discovered yet—it was an incredible experience! We all followed each other's accounts, then I ended up guest-starring in one of their Vines. After that, collaborations sort of just became a regular occurrence. We would schedule get-togethers where we'd team up to help each other make these fun videos and cross-promote to share our comical content with the world.

One day, this guy Jason Nash reached out to me and invited me to his house for a Vine he was shooting. If you don't know, Mr. Nash was at that time a forty-year-old Viner who had kids. So, for this skit, I pretended to be a kid in his children's room, where I was on a rocking horse, whining about needing better toys.

After we wrapped up, he said, "Okay, Manon, I'm going to have a party and I'm going to invite some other Vine people over so we can do a big meet-and-greet!"

"Great! That sounds like fun!" I said.

It was at the Jason Nash party that I met a bunch of very funny, talented women who liked to create, like me. But being in such a large group of people who pretty much all knew each other honestly made it feel like I had just started at a new high school all over again. I was nervous and didn't necessarily feel like I fit in yet, so I wasn't as outspoken as I normally am—which was a problem. During our almost-daily collaboration meetups, everyone took turns helping each other film their video ideas. And if you didn't have an idea or if you did and you didn't speak up about what you wanted to film, your project wouldn't get done that day. So, the fact that I wasn't outspoken meant that I was often featured in other people's videos rather than directing my own content ideas.

At the first house I visited to make a collab Vine, it was a bunch of girls wearing short shorts and low-cut shirts exposing their tatas, and me, the comedic relief. The Vine we did had salsa in it. The kind you eat, not the dance.

In my mind, I thought, *Am I supposed to just, like, be sexy right now? Because that's what everyone is doing...*

So, when the camera panned over to me, I just bit into the salsa-dipped tortilla chip with an obnoxious crunch and made a really goofy face after.

They all laughed, like it was the funniest thing they'd ever seen.

Oh, speaking of sexy things like skimpily dressed girls eating chips, the idea that "sex sells" was as prevalent in the world of Vine as it was in traditional media. That meant there were often times when some of the guy Viners only had girls in their videos for the purpose of being sexy. That was totally fine, but that's definitely *not* my comfort zone. My comfort zone is straight-up comedy. Nothing wrong with a person leading with their body; I just didn't. But now I do because this ASS is FIRE!

Collaborating with people who loved creating as much as I did was like being a kid again at a sleepover with my favorite friends, staying up all night laughing. It felt like improv camp, but we were filming this time around, and the way we were always having fun made it feel like we were in a constant state of play. That childlike sense of wonderment that I'd been trying to get back to since the complicated mess that was puberty for me had finally been actualized. And goofing off coupled with filming and editing made it feel like I'd stumbled into some fictional world where I'd joined a fun, creative version of wizard school.

In some ways, though, the world of Vine did have moments where it resembled the crappy aspects of high school. As in any group of people, there had to be someone who existed for the sole purpose of being the antagonist to all things positive. In our collective of creators, that was one of the biggest Viners at the time, whom I'll call "Amber."

Apparently, Amber actually pulled Jason aside at a function just to talk shit about me. It wasn't until after the party that he told me she said something along the lines of, "Don't help Manon with her content from now on..." Let me tell you, I'm very glad he waited until after the party to tell me that. Not that I was going to fight her or anything, but I would have loved to call her out on her bullshit for sure. Realistically I was still newly sober and quite sensitive, so when calling her out, I probably would have cried. Again. Gosh, I'm so cute.

Sometime later, I saw her at a film premiere and she came up to me to say hi. "Oh my God, do you eat at all?" was her greeting.

"Oh, that's nice... Hi to you too," was my response to that.

I saw her again one day at Café Gratitude. For those who aren't familiar with it, this café is a place where positivity is a part of the dining experience, so you have to order food in a particular way. Let's say you're getting quinoa and veggies and it's called something like Fortified. You have to order and be like, "I am fortified."

"*You ARE* fortified," is how they would respond, in a very Zen voice.

So, we're in this peaceful place that's all about gratitude, and Amber, along with another big Viner she was there with, approached our table.

I said something about being from Calabasas, to which Amber responded with, "Soooooo, basically you're a spoiled Kardashian?" Then she slid past me and bumped the back of my chair with her bootay, which led to my ribs getting pushed into the table. That made her laugh profusely.

Oh my gawd, what a sweetheart!

The universe must have been playing a cruel joke on me because I ran into her again at a party for an app launch. Just my luck. It was one of those events where the company invites all these influencers so that they'll come and hopefully post content as a means of promotion. I had a date with me. It was like a second date, too. Really, we weren't sure where we stood yet. But I had a cute crush on him and thought he was dreamy. This guy was also a Viner and a musician. Our Vine team-ups usually involved his playing the piano while I jokingly sang. Down the road, he went on to be on *American Idol* and *The Bachelor.*

Anyway, I went to this party with the musician and this other couple—who happened to be straight-edge—and when Amber came up to us, the first words out of her mouth were, "Are you four going to bang upstairs and have an orgy? Get up there already!"

We all literally said nothing and just stared at her. Not funny, not cool. Just weird.

Considering that every interaction that I had with her was not fun at all, I had the notion that she would not be someone I'd create with. I decided then that I was going to need to find my crew of people to Vine with, because creating with people like her around wasn't safe.

All of those experiences in conjunction with not making myself heard during collaborative sessions basically led to my opting to film Vines with close friends whom I felt really comfortable with—who I felt understood me and who got my sense of humor. I'm sure I could have grown a lot more had I kept collaborating with Vine legends who had twenty million followers. The opportunity was there, but the vibe wasn't quite right for me. And that's nothing against them, of course. There was just a certain energy I was going for and I couldn't find it with them.

After switching gears, I began Vining with people who were more my speed. It was another group of big-name creators, like Ry Doon, Jason Nash, Vincent Marcus, Jeff Cyrus, and Matt Cutshall. They were just a really, really amazing group of people that I had so much fun with and shared so, so many laughs with. Everything we created together felt like a hit. And there was always this constant high of creative energy when we teamed up. The days creating with them were some of the best days ever, and I became really close with all of them.

I remember meeting Vincent Marcus for the first time when we had to meet up to do an Old Navy holiday campaign. He came over, and we filmed a couple of Vines near my Christmas tree. Those few six-second bits led to hours of laughing for us. To this day, I will still create with Vincent, because he's just such an awesome person. Sometimes I forget how talented my friends are.

I also had many giggle-filled experiences with Jeff Cyrus. He is one of the most talented guys on the planet and should have a trillion followers, in my opinion. The first time we spent hours laughing was at Coachella. Just hours of running around improvising back and forth. We then went on to make hilarious Vines that still make me crack up to this day. There is something so special about having that creative synergy with someone who just gets it like you do.

A similar thing happened with the lovely Matt Cutshall. He and I got together at a Coffee Bean to shoot a Vine campaign for their company and clicked right away, laughing more than working.

From that point on, Matt and I got together pretty often to create content and quickly developed a friendship founded on silliness and incessant laughter. All good friends have running jokes. Ours was a series that we Vined where I would pretend to have feelings for him and just completely overdo it, then he would always basically have to push me off. That story line went on until the end of Vine. What was hard about that was our Vine crew was composed of really, really good actors, so things often came off too realistic. To some, it was probably like viewers were watching these mini reality shows and couldn't discern what was real and what wasn't. I can't begin to count how many times people thought I was dating some guy whom I costarred in Vines with. That happened to all of us, really.

If you were on Vine, you know Matt Cutshall would film a lot with Arielle Vandenberg, pretty much the only person other than me that he'd team up with for a good chunk of time. Back then, they were really good friends, but he confided in me that he had such strong feelings for her. And not being with her burdened him with heartache. I helped him through that as best I could. Having followers start picking sides with the whole Team Manon/Team Arielle thing didn't make that any easier.

When the fan-made rivalry started popping up in comments, I was just like, *This is ridiculous… There are no teams! I'm on Arielle's team! I'm not trying to do anything. I'm just trying to make fun, captivating content for entertainment purposes, not for gossip!*

Skip ahead a few years later to a day when I went over to Matt's house to make a video. Arielle was there, so when Matt left to go pick up some grub, Arielle and I got to talking.

"I'm seeing someone," she said, grinning.

"No way! Who?" I asked.

"Matt!"

[Insert cheer and hugs here]

I pretty much freaked out because I was so happy; their becoming a couple was such a long time coming. We ALL wanted it because their chemistry is undeniable and beautiful to witness! But I suppose it was all about timing for them.

It's proof that whatever is meant to be will be. And if it IS supposed to happen, you really can't mess it up. Sometimes you just have to wait and what's meant to happen will happen.

It's actually crazy how so many lives were changed by an app meant to churn out six-second loops. So many friendships were forged. Some of my best friends came from that app! In the case of Arielle and Matt, love was made possible. It launched so many careers and brand deals. It not only changed so many lives, but it changed social media and the internet forever.

And then, like all things, it just freaking died.

9

Fruits of the Vine

Flash back to two years before Vine prematurely perished. An opportunity arose for me to travel to the Gold Coast in Brisbane, Australia, to be an extra on *Pirates of the Caribbean: Dead Men Tell No Tales*. There were a bunch of other influencers there. The production required hundreds of extras, who would all get there at 4:00 A.M. for makeup. You wouldn't think they'd go all out for makeup on extras, but the work they did was incredible. We got lucky and got to stroll in around 9:00 A.M., after the mayhem.

"Okay, so, unfortunately, you're not going to get to meet any of the cast or take pictures with them, but you can take a picture with this Johnny Depp cardboard cutout..." said the marketing manager.

Um... what? Why go all the way to Australia to take a picture with a piece of cardboard, which I could've just done in my bedroom? Not that I have a life-size Johnny Depp cutout at home. I don't! I have one of Tom Hardy, and it's wonderful.

What am I, sixteen?

I wish...

While I was on set with my pirate-era-appropriate makeup, a spectacularly beautiful, 18th century–style dress, and a fun hat, I decided to film a Vine outside of a porta-potty. I asked a PA to pretend to be my assistant and, in the voice of a diva, said, "Open my trailer door, Jacob... " or something to that effect.

As I was filming, Mr. Depp walked by, stopped there abruptly, and then just stared at me.

And I just stared back at him for a while, thinking, *Oh shit...*

I was so caught off guard. Disney had said we weren't going to meet him, so I hadn't planned out what'd I'd say if I actually met him. Then I kind of had it in my head that I wasn't supposed to talk to him at all. So there was a prolonged silence.

After what felt like a long dueling stare-down, I pointed at the porta-potty. "Oh, I'm just going to my trailer," is what eventually came out of my mouth.

He paused and stared at me for a bit. "That used to be my trailer," he said coolly.

Then I giggled like a little schoolgirl. I did so in the most over-the-top way possible too.

He smiled and nodded his head, then walked off very casually.

I hurried on back to where all of the other influencers were and I played it very cool. "OH MY GOD! GUESS WHO I JUST GOT TO TALK TO! JOHNNY DEPP!"

After gabbing on about the experience, I finished filming my Vine, then the influencers and I gathered together to take a group photo. That's when the Depp came strolling through, all dressed up in his Jack Sparrow garb, and joined in on the freaking group photo! And I promise you it wasn't just a guy hiding behind the cardboard cutout. At least, I'm 90 percent confident it wasn't. Check my Instagram just to make sure.

Following our photo shoot, we all got to watch him work and sword-fight and do his Sparrow thang. The campaign was incredible, but the funny thing is, the whole purpose of this particular campaign with Disney was to record during production, then promote the movie on Vine and post content on social media at the time of its release. Well, Vine was still alive during the filming of *Dead Men Tell No Tales*. TWO freaking *years* later, when the movie was finally released, Vine was dead and gone. At least I still got to post some photos on Instagram.

The same group of influencers who got to be extras on set got to go to the Shanghai Disneyland Hotel in China for the premiere of the film. We got to tour around the area and experience foreign cuisine. Though everyone actually ended up going to McDonald's on our exploring day. Let's talk about how disappointing that was, being the only one who wanted authentic Chinese food. Needless to say, I was pissed. I mean, McDonald's was fine and all, but come on… No, it wasn't fine. I'm still annoyed.

Anyway, us influencers were on the red carpet with Johnny Depp, Orlando Bloom, Javier Bardem, the rest of the main cast of the movie, and *nobody else*. There were thousands of Chinese fans asking us for autographs. I wasn't about to burst their bubble and disclose that we weren't in the movie, so we signed stuff anyway and let people take photos of us like we were A-listers. Which I have been anyway for years now (in my head). I've actually never felt different from super-famous actors. I guess it goes back to the fact that I feel we are all truly connected.

For anyone aspiring to be social media famous, here's a lesson for you: Even social media platforms themselves may only get fifteen minutes of fame. If the app or site doesn't die out, its algorithm might change on you and you won't have the same reach you used to. Ads may one day pay you less, or maybe nothing at all. If you're only focusing your efforts on one platform, you'll be screwed if things tilt out of your favor.

Vine built many careers. We all thought it'd last for decades. Then, *boom.* Gone. What killed it, you might ask. Instagram's fifteen-second videos might have signaled the beginning of the end. And Facebook videos. Then Instagram videos got bumped up to a sixty-second limit. The 'Gram also drew attention to celebrity accounts with the Explore page. All of that must have enticed advertisers to spend their money there instead of on Vine. And where the marketing money went, the Vine stars went.

I read in an article that said some of the top Viners had gone all self-preservation mode and asked for something like $1 million each in order to keep producing content for the platform. And when they didn't get that, they basically said, "Okay, then we're leaving." Their loyal audiences followed, probably hoping to enjoy longer content from their favorite creators, which is totally understandable.

The rest of us got kind of screwed, because we didn't know about this big negotiation, so we had no idea Vine was about to wither away. Not that it mattered, I guess. More of us demanding compensation probably wouldn't have made them say yes. Unless Vine was hoping those of us who were still on the platform were going to pick up the slack, which clearly didn't happen either, though I tried.

Vine's ending was so abrupt.

After it had kind of left the building, I didn't really promote my other platforms as much as I used to promote Vine. Instagram and Facebook required more long-form content that took a little more effort, which meant more work when it came to collaborations and more sophisticated recording equipment.

Not all three million of my followers organically transferred over to Facebook and Instagram, but at least a good chunk did. For the sake of being candid, not having the following I used to was disheartening. Comparing and despairing left me feeling like I didn't measure up to what I once had been. But I had to take solace in the fact that I was lucky enough to still have brand deals and to still have those followers who'd migrated over to my other accounts. I was so incredibly grateful that fans of my brand of humor sought me out elsewhere. So, if you OG fans from Vine are reading this, thank you so much! I appreciate you more than you'll ever know.

Now that I was sans a few million followers, I more or less had to start over with a new pair of eyes. Could I be more than a Vine star?

Okay, longer-form videos for Instagram. I need to write skits. Keep making videos. Keep creating. Keep making content.

Perseverance is key for anyone who wants to keep a footing in the world of social media. Perseverance and frequency. Keep creating. Do it often and regularly.

So, that's exactly what I did. At one point, just for shits and giggles, I posted a video on Facebook where I rapped to a Ying Yang Twins song called "What's Happnin!" I loved that freaking song when I was fifteen, so when it randomly came on my playlist, I thought, *I should just lip-sync/rap the hell out of this in the car.* I did it in one take, posted it, and it got over seventy-five million views on Facebook. People love watching people who aren't dancers or rappers when they attempt to dance and rap for some reason. And when it's a super-white girl with crunk moves, it puts a comedic spin on things. Plus, the Ying Yang Twins gave me their approval by reposting it on their page. All in all, a win!

Love you, Twins!

For me, I kept doing my job as an actor and a producer creating content because I loved doing it, not because I was trying to have a career. But doing what I loved full-time was the dream. Having an income stream from my creative work is just the cherry on top.

Thankfully, with the following I built, I got lucky enough to work with a bunch of brands before the death of Vine, deals that continued to keep coming my way after it was gone. I had the opportunity to work with brands like Best Buy, Nordstrom, Amazon, T-Mobile... the list goes on and on. Through the brand work, I was able to do what I loved, like writing, directing, and starring in online commercials.

As an actor, it's tough landing any kind of gig. You're lucky if you even get a callback or are brought in for commercials. The odds are just really stacked against us actors here in LA because there are just too many of us vying for work. I had no right to feel bummed about losing my following when my past creative endeavors granted me the gift of opportunities to create and direct like I used to when I was a kid, even in the absence of the app that changed my life. And I have so much gratitude for that.

Some deals had really amazing perks that brought about such memorable experiences, some of which I got to share with those I love. For instance, with Bud Light I got to go to Super Bowl 50. The best part about it is I got to bring my dad with me to San Francisco for the game! We made Vines together on the bus. My dad cracks me up when he acts. I love directing him because his goofball side really shows up. I think he secretly wanted to be an actor back in the day.

(Psst, YOU STILL CAN BE, DAD.)

Like I said, I'll be right here, cheering you on!

I also went to Chicago and New York a bunch of times for Twitter and to promote TV shows. Oh, and one of those trips to New York City changed the trajectory of my life forever (but I'll get to that later). There were a few years in a row when I was literally traveling on around forty planes a year. Which is an insane amount for little ol' me.

Brand deals, that movie, and travel aside, the best fruit I plucked from the Vine is the fact that I met so many people from that app who have played such a crucial part in my life and creativity. I've met so many talented people who make me laugh. And if you haven't gotten the message by now, laughter is my number one value. I know people value it. But it's my top value. I absolutely *need* laughter in my life. It's the medicine that keeps me light in what can feel like a heavy world at times.

So, this chapter is my ode to the people who created Vine, those whom I had the pleasure of creating content with on that app, the friends I've made because of it, and all of the people who have followed me over the years and made all of this possible.

Thanks! And cheers!

Did that sound like the end of the book? It's not. There's still more ahead so, uh… go grab a hot tea and then turn the page!

10

Speaking Your Truth

A SOULMATE IS SOMEONE whom you share a powerful, magnetic connection with. It's instant and undeniable. It's a natural affinity that, once found, completes you—you're finally part of a matching pair. Your soulmate is someone you might possibly even marry.

A twin flame is basically two flames from the same candle. It doesn't necessarily have to be something romantic. Twin flames are more about a breathtaking connection filled with synchronicities based on commonalities from your pasts. Resonance. It's two people who teach each other things, help each other to grow and heal. It's someone whom, when you meet, you feel instantly comfortable with, like you've known each other since the toddler days. It wasn't until I met my best friend Travis that I understood what that meant.

As I mentioned earlier, I met Travis at Second City in class level one back in 2010. Twenty-one-year-old me walked in and locked eyes with this blue-eyed John Travolta–looking guy, and instantly, my heart dropped. The whole world freaking stopped. My body felt, like, different.

Oh my God! Who is this man? I feel like I know him deeply, I thought.

He has mentioned many times since then that he had a similar response to his first sight of me in my purple pants. I think our souls were bonding.

After we met, we'd hang before and after every class. I felt like I was thinking about him a lot. When I watched him perform, I would just die laughing. The same thing happened to him when he observed my performances. Oh, and when we performed together? It was a volatile mix, because we would always break character and end up laughing so damn hard! Think funny *Saturday Night Live* skits where two cast members find each other too hilarious to keep a straight face even when they're not at the funny part of the scene yet. The teacher would literally not even put us together to perform after a while because we kept breaking into this infectious laughter that would get the whole class going hysterically, like someone was pumping laughing gas in through the vents.

When Vine happened, he and I filmed a lot together. There was never a dull moment, as you can imagine. And he's super talented, so it always made creating so much easier. We're still very, very close to this day. I doubt that'll ever change. Travis is family. A best friend from a past life. I love that kid and I'd die for him. Or more likely die laughing because of him.

He and I are so tight that I had this man in my wedding party as a... bridesmaid? No... bridesman? Yeah, that.

It's good to have those kinds of relationships. Longevity in relationships is something I dearly appreciate. Travis knew me before I got sober. He's seen me at my worst. He's seen me at my best. And when a friend sticks around through the good and bad, when they're there for you like you're there for them, when they show up when it counts and when it doesn't, that's how you know a friendship is true.

There was a night back when I was a year or two sober where he wanted to hang out. Now, "hanging out" in this context meant he and some people going out drinking, and I wasn't about that. A debate waged on in my head about whether or not I should tell him that I didn't want to be around him while he was drunk or drinking. Nothing against anyone who drinks, but after becoming sober, being around drunks wasn't my favorite.

When I finally gained the courage to talk with him about his drinking one night, I said, "I don't want to hang out with you when you drink, it's unattractive to me."

Boy, he did not like that at all.

So, you know, to show me up, he went out that night and bought a jumbo bottle of white wine and drank the whole damn thing. His way of basically saying, "*Eff off, you don't know anything, Manon. I'm still awesome when I drink.*"

The next day, I got a call from him telling me he was done drinking. And that was when he stopped drinking. He hasn't had a drink since!

I firmly believe that when you speak your truth, you are helping other people. When we're true to ourselves, it benefits the people around us. It's not always the most comfortable thing in the world to set boundaries in the moment and to tell a harsh truth to someone we're cool with or a relative, but, based on the experiences that I have had, I do believe that it's the most helpful thing and everybody needs to hear what truth it is you need to share. To be honest, I think we could all use more of this. I know I sure as hell appreciate when people tell me how my actions affect them, even if it's negative, because it inspires me to grow and makes me want to become better.

People are tiptoeing around each other *far too much* these days. Whether it's how we feel about someone or an area where someone can improve, we often don't tell people what they need to hear because we're scared of not being liked or hurting someone's feelings. We've stopped challenging each other to grow. As long as your truth comes from a place of love, only good can come from it.

Speaking my truth has without a doubt helped me with setting boundaries. Learning to have boundaries has been a very interesting journey for me. I actually had to read a book called *Boundaries* because I didn't really have any with men… or my family, or ANYONE. I was always too afraid to make someone uncomfortable or hurt their feelings.

I remember when my sponsor told me, "Girl, we gotta teach you how to set firm boundaries. When a man approaches you and you're NOT interested, 'No' is a complete sentence. You don't need an explanation. You're allowed to say, '*Thanks, I'm flattered, but no thank you.*' You're allowed to decline."

Whaaaat???

That was a *huge* freaking moment for me, because before that, I would always make sure to people-please. I hated confrontation so much that I would give out my number to guys I had no intention of getting to know or going out with, then I would spend two weeks trying to dodge their calls and ghosting their texts. We've all been there, right, lady readers? I mean, I'm sure some guys have been there too, let's be honest.

For anyone who doesn't want to shut down someone who had the guts to ask for their number, we say yes when we don't want to as a means to perhaps create harmony in the moment and not offend anyone by straight-up rejecting their offer to connect. But guess what? A no right away is better than days and weeks of blowing them off. Then you're just spreading unnecessary anxiety and stress to others, and possibly confirming the idea that all people suck.

Here's what my sponsor went on to say about saying yes when you know you want to say no: "Everyone deserves love. And if it's not you, allow the person you're not interested in to shut the door on you so they can have the opportunity to open their energy to somebody else."

I realized that what I was doing was not only not helping them find their love or their next connection or whatever, it was actually inhibiting them. Wasting their energy. Once I learned that what was best for them was for me to say no if my answer was no, I started practicing that and establishing boundaries.

We all need boundaries and structures to help us flow smoothly through life, because we do well within a container that's suited for us. When I say "container," think of it as a mobile home for the self that allows you to navigate the world in a way where you feel safe and comfortable. Even though it hurts and it sucks, I think we respect when others set their boundaries and make them known.

A lot of the strength I have now comes from people who have come before me, mainly strong, intelligent women. There was one instance where I had a crush on this guy who was kind of like a friend… I mean, he was a friend. This guy—let's call him Jacob— would always do things like pay for my meals and get my door and walk me to the car after we hung out. Jacob was pretty gentlemanly but also pretty flirtatious at times, so I assumed, *Oh, he must have feelings! But… he has a long-term girlfriend, so what's going on there?*

Being uncertain about his feelings and motives left me tormented. My sponsor helped me through the situation.

"What do I do?" I asked her.

"Why don't you ask for clarity on the matter?"

"… What do you mean?"

"Why don't you ask him, '*Hey, are you flirting with me?*' Get insight on whether he has feelings for you or not."

"No way! That's the scariest thing in the world. I'll look so stupid."

I could never just do that. Right? Like, I didn't have the courage to be vulnerable and to go first in those situations, *especially* not without alcohol.

So, this woman walked me through it and I let her advice simmer.

Later on, I had coffee with the flirtatious gentleman named Jacob. This cute guy with an adorable energy and demeanor was sitting across from me, and I remember saying something along the lines of, "Hey… so… sometimes I get a flirtatious vibe from you and it makes me feel feelings… And I want to check in and see if you actually do have feelings for me or not." (You're reading my line in Kristen Stewart's voice because I called this guy Jacob, aren't you?)

My heart... it was beating so damn fast! Because I'd never said anything like that before without it being provoked by something a guy said or did. I'd always play it cool and wait for them to lead. Or I would text something like that to probe without the anxiety of the face-to-face. You know, because millennial.

Until this point, I didn't know that I could take the lead or go first. Society, film, and television always make it seem like only the man can lead.

So, I asked him this, and his eyes got all wide. He just stared for a few moments before he finally said something: "Oh my God... Oh my God..."

"What? What?" I said, panicking.

"I just... maybe I've been very selfish."

"What do you mean?"

"I think I just get something from you that I don't get from my current girlfriend... and I'm really sorry for that."

"That's fine... Thank you for saying that... So... you don't have feelings? Can you tell me that you don't have feelings?"

He just sat there, silent.

"It would be really helpful to know if you don't have feelings... Because if you don't have feelings, then my feelings will definitely dissolve. I'm not really into people that aren't into me."

He. Still. Couldn't. Answer.

I just kind of let Jacob sit there for a while. Not long after, I hugged him goodbye and I got in my car. As he walked away, I saw him wipe his eyes.

Wait... Is he crying?

The next thing I knew, I was bawling my eyes out in my car. I cried because I'd expressed myself. I had taken the lead and asked for clarity. I felt I had bravely reclaimed my power by using my voice. I had discovered that I could get information for myself; I didn't have to go through life with unanswered questions.

The unknown makes us uncomfortable. It's the uncertainty that scares us. It's a major source of anxiety for most people. To cope with the absence of answers, we start storytelling—making up stories about situations. The Landmark Forum talks about how "there's what happens in life and then there's the story that we create about what happened."

Oftentimes, it is just that. A story. Not actual truth.

A week after I sat down with Jacob, he texted me saying something along the lines of: *Hey. Just so you know I'm going to work on things with my girlfriend. You made me realize that we weren't in a great spot and I appreciate you for that.*

When I reflect upon my friend quitting drinking and Jacob working things out with his girlfriend after confronting them about my feelings, I think not of how my raw honesty may or may have not played a part in contributing to their personal development, but instead I think of how those experiences empowered me to feel comfortable with being able to share my truth and how it taught me that it's okay to speak my mind if it comes from a good, caring place. Speaking up is something that's difficult for most of us. And after witnessing how being straight-up with those two might have steered them in the right direction, and after realizing that they didn't hate me for being honest, I gained the positive reinforcement I needed to be okay with being open with others.

Anyway, from that moment on, I was able to release the kind of jittery obsession I had with not knowing where Jacob and I stood or if something was going to ever happen between us. That connects back to how when we're honest with ourselves and we lead with our hearts and our vulnerability, things work out.

Something similar happened with this guy from the Groundlings improv school. The Groundlings Theatre is an improv hot spot in Los

Angeles that birthed legends like Lisa Kudrow and Kristen Wiig. The guy's name was Carter, and he happened to be fifteen years older than I was. We got together in class once to write some scenes for an assignment. I felt a strong and sweet connection between us pretty much right off the bat. It was just my luck that this guy had a girlfriend too.

Why am I running into these people with girlfriends? They are all freakin' taken! What's going on with me? Why am I attracting people who are unavailable? Do I not feel like I deserve the love I've always dreamed of? I always like to ask myself if I'm deserving of the types of people that come into my life, because water seeks its own level. Sooo, what was going on?

If I respond to this situation differently, I will get a different outcome. Or so I've be told.

In my early twenties, I didn't care if a guy had a girlfriend. My mentality was, *If they're giving me attention, I don't care if they have a girlfriend or if they're married or whatever! Just give me the attention!* Because I was that insecure, you know? The attention was like a drug to me. But after I did some deep spiritual work, that type of behavior wasn't going to cut it anymore. It profoundly affected my self-esteem in the long run and was probably why I was attracting less than ideal partners.

So, at this point with Carter, I was functioning differently. I was aware of my actions. I was feeling things. I was not crossing the lines young Mannie would have.

Now, Carter was a very spiritually connected dude. Being that he was older, he was a lot more present, which helped me to get out of being on my phone so often. With him, I felt all of the same things I had felt with Jacob and more. *Oooooh, I have feelings for him! But he has a girlfriend!*

After the final class ended, he wanted to continue hanging out. He framed it in a way that made it seem harmless.

Trembling, I said, "I would love to keep spending time with you, but unfortunately, you have a girlfriend and I'm feeling feelings, and I don't need another friend that I have feelings for in my life right now, so best of luck."

Carter just stared at me like a deer in headlights, like, "*HUH?*" I get it. I probably came across like a nut bag, especially because we didn't know each other that well. Sure, I could've avoided addressing the feelings I was having, but I felt compelled to be honest and to share my heart. It was a risk for sure.

After Carter's brain rebooted, he finally said, "Thank you for your honesty." And then he left.

And, just like that, I was free from those feelings! Because I'd claimed my power and told my truth. Nothing left to hold on to!

When we tell our truth, we're free of the weight it imposes on our thoughts. The less we have to think about, the lighter we feel. I didn't need Carter to respond. I needed me to be in my power and unburdened by uncertainty.

After that, I didn't think about it anymore. I had written him off. I thought that all the possibilities were gone from that relationship. So, I went about my life. I went on a trip to London, worked on my craft. Then, two months later, I got a call from Carter.

"Hey, Manon. I just wanted to let you know that my relationship ended a month ago and I'd like to take you out, if you're interested."

"Wow… Okay. Yeah!"

The air was clear, neither of us had any baggage, and now we were able to start exploring our feelings with a clean slate.

One of the greatest lessons that I've ever learned is that things tend to work out more smoothly for those who remember to take care of themselves. Took me twenty-seven years, but I had finally figured that out!

I feel like my journey has been one of reclaiming my power as a woman and using my voice, not apologizing for it. Owning my own feelings without putting them on other people. Taking care of myself. Telling men that I can't spend time with them if they are in a relationship because I've developed feelings for them. That's me taking care of myself rather than putting myself in a situation where it can never really turn out the way that I want it to deep in my heart. That's how so many heartaches start. Because if my glass is filled with dirty water and I want clean water, then I have to dump out the dirty water to make room for it. I believe energy works the same way.

If you're curious about what happened with me and Carter, we ended up being together for a little over a year. He was really wonderful. We became really good friends. Ultimately, I think that the age difference, as much as I didn't like to admit it, affected us. I hadn't even entered my thirties, and he was already out of his.

Eventually, we broke things off because I had decided to move across the country to New York City.

11

Manon and the City

I NEVER WANTED to live in New York. The first time I ever visited there was in ninth grade for our school's varsity choir's performance. Not for a performance I was in or anything, I just went to hang with my bestie Tara. We walked around doing all of the touristy things you could imagine. We had authentic New York–style pizza (which was mandatory after hearing *so* much about it). We visited Ground Zero. We went on a cruise around Manhattan and danced the night away. We went to the wax museum and took pictures of all the fake celebs on our disposable cameras. If social media had been a thing then, I would have been ALL OVER IT at fourteen! Glad it wasn't…

Overall, it was a good time, but living there just didn't seem as appealing as on *Sex and the City*.

After that, I didn't end up going back to New York until six years later, with Danielle, after I quit my job at Daily Grill. As an older, more aware Manon, I remember feeling very overwhelmed by the people and the energy in New York during that trip, thinking, *I don't know how anyone could ever live here. I could never. I need things spread out. I need nature.*

During the year I dated Carter, he would always talk about New York, like obsessively longing for it. He had lived there for fourteen years and he must have friggin' missed it, because somehow he managed to bring up New York City in every conversation. Now that I think about it, he actually might have programmed me to move there.

After Carter, I landed a gig writing and starring in a commercial for PiperWai—a natural charcoal deodorant company that started on *Shark*

Tank. Our writing session was in a Dominican Republic tree house where we went ziplining all day. Tough stuff! Got so much work done... Not! But I did get bitten by thirty-eight mosquitoes, so that's dope! When the writing was complete, there was a launch party in New York City for this five-minute commercial that was featured on Facebook. Guess who I spotted there?

Did you say Matt LeBlanc? No, but close!

It was Ross from *Friends*, David Schwimmer himself! I tell people that I played it cool, but I assure you, I did not. I was shaking with excitement. I mean, the day Jennifer Aniston followed me on Instagram makes the list of one of the best days of my life, because she's just darling and she's a huge inspiration to me. If I freaked out about that, meeting one of the cast members of my favorite show of all time in PERSON obviously led to an even bigger freak-out!

I pulled myself together and went on over to introduce myself to him. "David? Hi! I'm Manon Math—"

"I know who you are," David Schwimmer said in response, a warm smile on his face. "You're very funny. I watched your stand-up. I love how you dance onstage during your set; it's pretty hilarious!"

That, I was not expecting...

He and I talked for twenty memorable minutes, and I got to tell him how powerful *Friends* was for me. I told him that I'd gotten to see a live filming of *Friends* once with my friend Alexis. It was the season seven episode with Denise Richards where she whips her hair back and forth. Schwimmer and I bonded over the difference between being in LA, where you live in a box and then drive from place to place solo, versus being in New York, where you're just with everybody the second you step out your door and you pretty much walk everywhere.

Meeting him felt like a sign to me. Later on, during that visit, I took a walk through Madison Square Park, right next to Shake Shack. It felt like a movie. Probably because a lot of movies were filmed there, like *Something Borrowed*. As I was walking along, thinking about meeting

David Schwimmer, something came over me and this thought popped into my head:

Oh, I need to live here. Wait... okay, me and Ross are going to become friends. We're going to get lunch! It's a great idea!

(Didn't happen.)

The idea of moving there was interesting to me because I had never thought about it before that moment. At the time, part of me was feeling stagnant and stuck living in Los Angeles. I mean, I'd been there since birth. Twenty-eight years of living in the same place. Despite getting to travel, I was yearning for a more permanent change to mix things up. I was too comfortable in LA. I think I was always a little envious of the people who had moved to Los Angeles from their hometowns. I wanted to be courageous too! I wanted to be outside of my comfort zone for once.

Not long after I returned from that trip, I ended things with Carter, a man I loved, so I could be on my own. Sure, I cared about him a lot, but he didn't feel like the *ONE*. And in order to find the one, I had to let go of whoever was not the one, to empty my cup to make room for the one to come in. And that was really hard for me, because I was used to breaking up with people because the relationship was toxic. Like, if there was yelling or alcohol it was easier to walk away because it was easier to get real with myself and say, *Look how detrimental this relationship is...* But to walk away from a great relationship with Carter where we got along really well? That was hard, weird, and uncomfortable. And it didn't really make sense, but I just had to trust my gut and move forward.

So, I moved to New York on August 13, 2017. I had found this Airbnb type of place in the East Village, the very same neighborhood where I'd met Schwimmer.

Oh, we're definitely going to be friends now!

Nope.

Plot twist: I never actually saw "Ross" again.

The landlord who rented this place to me was this tall, skinny Asian dude who always seemed to be sweating profusely when it wasn't really even that hot at the time. He might have been on drugs or something. The idea that he might have been high on something didn't really click until there was this kerfuffle with a payment three months in and we ended up in this weird text back-and-forth thing when I decided to leave. He started talking about the fact that I could call my lawyers. When we spoke in person, he asked me if I was wearing a wire.

I was like, *Okay, this guy is on drugs, because I'm just letting him know that I'm leaving and he thinks I'm an informant or something.*

When I made it clear that I wanted to leave, he kept trying to convince me to keep living there. He begged me to stay for two more months. I said, "All right, fine."

Then, the next day, he said, "Okay, I do need you to move out." *Make up your mind!*

The landlord was just so all over the place that it kind of inspired me to get my own place that had *my* name on the lease. Something more… *legitimate* than the wannabe Airbnb I'd been staying at. But in New York, if you get your own place, you have to make a certain amount of money. Like, a stupid amount of money. And if you don't, you have to get someone to cosign your lease.

If I'm really going to do this, I'm going to have to do this for at least a year, I thought during my apartment hunt.

When I'd first moved to the Big Apple, I was like, *I'm only going to go for three months.*

And after a few weeks there, I loved it so much, I told myself, *I'll stay here for six months!*

Then at the three-month mark, I thought, *A year it is!*

I ended up finding this dreamscape of an apartment in Gramercy on Twenty-Fifth Street and Third Avenue. Cosigner issues aside, I was so very glad that I had saved enough to be able to afford to live in this place. It was a really cute one-bedroom with exposed-brick walls, which I always thought to be aesthetically appealing. There was a washer and dryer in the unit, which makes you like royalty in the city.

Oh, right before that move I immediately hopped on Bumble, swiped a few times, and found this guy named Christian—a gorgeous, mid-thirties Puerto Rican firefighter who I thought was super cute. His eyes were this beautiful blue and I smiled the second I saw him.

Christian and I met on a rainy Tuesday night. I saw Marianne Williamson speak live at the Marble Collegiate Church and then met up with him after. Halfway through the dinner, he admitted that he had he followed me on Vine and that he was a huge fan. I was flattered. Now, usually, I don't love to be romantically involved with a fan. But he had a really easygoing energy and we laughed a lot. And if you can make me laugh, then you basically have an in to win over my heart.

Christian rode a motorcycle, so when we went out together, I would ride on the back with him all over Brooklyn and Manhattan, and he took me to a lot of fun spots. It was really romantic. He was like a modern-day Aladdin showing Jasmine around the world on a flying carpet, except for us it was a motorized bike around the "world" of New York City.

He and I dated for a while, and then one night, he asked to be exclusive. It was time for me to listen through the quiet, to be so open and meditate on what I was feeling in the moment. I remember lying in bed thinking, *You know... I just got out of a relationship with Carter a few months back... I just moved to New York...* My heart then gave me my answer. *I'm not ready to be exclusive.*

So, I told him just that. I asked instead if we could still be open. And it was a *HUGE* deal for me to set that boundary, because at the time, I was so used to just people-pleasing, like, "Oh, you want to be in a relationship? Okay, fine! Sure! I'll be your girlfriend!" Because I was afraid that I'd lose them if I said what I really wanted, whether that was staying open, as in this case, or breaking things off because I was unsure about them. It was different for me to express that. Before this point, I usually hadn't owned what I wanted.

Christian was totally respectful about it all. "Hey, that sounds great," he responded. "I might take a step back from this, but I would still like to see you because I enjoy your company."

After Christian, there was Samuel, who, like Carter, was older than me, but not by as much. We met at ANOTHER Marianne Williamson lecture on *A Course in Miracles.* Earlier that day, my friend Katie had told me about these blue-light-blocking glasses that helped you sleep better. That night, on the way to the lecture, I saw these two tall men dressed in black and wearing glasses, looking like they were in *The Matrix.*

Oh, they're handsome, I thought. *Wait... are they wearing those blue-light-blocking glasses that my friend Katie was JUST talking about?*

On the way out of Marianne Williamson's speech, before the questions began, I was walking down the stairs and the guys were right next to me. "Hey," I said, "by chance, are those blue-light-blocking glasses?"

"Yes," Samuel responded in an Australian accent. Then he smiled. "I actually created these. Would you like me to send you a pair?"

We exchanged numbers, then a few days later, he sent me a pair. Not long after, we ended up getting together for a green juice to talk about potentially having me promote his glasses. We ended up not talking about that; we talked about other stuff. We talked a lot about travel, as we both did a lot of it. We connected over our love of self-improvement and spiritual workshops. I remember feeling a strong connection between us pretty quickly. Later, he asked me to lunch and we ended up spending twelve magical hours together gallivanting around Manhattan. We got cupcakes, enjoyed amazing meals together, listened to music, got foot rubs—all sorts of fun stuff around the city.

By the end of the night, I thought, *I should probably sleep with him, because if I don't do it now my husband is going to come and I'm not going to get the opportunity…* (WTF?)

I said good night to Samuel and headed up to my apartment. That thought rattled around in my head all the way until I got to my door. Then I texted him, telling him to come up. He did. And we got physical.

I'm not sure if all Australians are as domineering and vulgar about sex as he was, but he was a bit dominating for my taste, so I automatically put him in the category of just another sexual partner, not someone who could protect my heart.

As we lay there together, this sadness rushed over me. *Oh, this isn't going to be a reoccurring thing… I'm not going to be able to be with him again,* I thought. I was sad because even though the sex was a little bit dominating, it was erotic and I was attracted to Samuel.

That sadness must have shown up on my face or something, because when Samuel looked at me, he said, "What's going on? What are you thinking about?"

"Oh, I guess I'm sad because this is going to be the last time you and I do this."

His eyes widened. "What? Why? Am I not a potential partner because I travel a lot?"

"I don't know. That could be part of it…"

"What is it then?"

"I don't know… I think it's because I feel like my husband is coming." *Why did I just say that?!*

His jaw dropped. His eyes widened further as his brows rose. "What?! You're married?!"

"No! No, no! Sorry! My husband and I haven't met yet; I just feel like he's coming." *Manon, what the eff! You probably sound like a lunatic! Why are you saying that your husband is coming? You haven't even met the guy yet!*

SHUT UP! But I couldn't help the words coming out of my mouth. They were just spilling out whether I liked it or not.

Samuel smiled. Then he left.

A week later, he FaceTimed me, saying that he'd like clarity on why I felt the way I did. I remember thinking I could do one of two things. I could lie and say, "*I don't know... I didn't mean it. Forget it.*" Or I could tell the truth.

So I decided, *You know what? When I say what's helpful to me, it helps other people.*

"The truth is that I felt a little bit dominated by you and it wasn't as intimate as I would have preferred," I said with a sigh. "I felt far from you. And that to me felt like something I didn't want to get close to."

It was clear by his face that he was really taking that all in.

Months and months later, we got together for breakfast. At one point, he reached across the table and grabbed my hand. "You've made a profound difference in my life," he said, emotion in his voice. Mind you, Samuel was very, very logical and never came off as emotional whatsoever. "I've recently reconnected with an ex-girlfriend and asked her if she felt the same way you did. And she pretty much said the same thing you said. Because of the information you gave me, I went to Bali and took an intimacy workshop." He'd gotten back together with his ex. He said, "My ex-girlfriend reported to me that the sex has been so much better and more intimate, so thank you for your honesty."

Dating relationships aside, during my time in New York, I made some really good friends. I befriended an event producer named Noel. I made best friends with this adorable blond beauty named Carrie. I was crying outside of a twelve-step meeting. It was just one of those days where I was in a new city and I just felt super alone and disconnected. So I was sitting on the steps letting my emotions flow, and this gal dressed in a flannel came up to me, cookies in hand, and comforted me. "You should come to this meeting I go to tomorrow.

It's a spiritual workshop that we have Sunday mornings," she said. Then she gave me her number.

I went to the meeting, then afterward, Carrie and I spent the whole day together, skipping around the city, sitting in Washington Square Park, telling each other secrets, getting French fries.

She was a stable influence for me, someone who served as a home base of sorts, helping me ground myself while I was in a city that was unfamiliar. She became one of the familiar things! We quickly became best friends. We grew so close that she ended up actually being in my wedding.

Another friend I made was this cool gal named Chelsi. She really played a big part in helping me get in my feminine energy. She's an S Factor teacher, meaning she teaches pole dancing. But it's more than a remarkable stripper talent, it's about helping women be comfortable in their bodies. Yes! Please! More! Thank you!

Chelsi also taught me about loving everything around you—in other words, only having things in your home that spark joy. Kind of like the whole Marie Kondo thing where she talks about how you should "Keep only those things that speak to your heart. Then take the plunge and discard all the rest. By doing this, you can reset your life and embark on a new lifestyle."

Chelsi once said, "I'm obsessed with and love everything in my apartment!"

I was like, "Wait, what? What does that feel like?"

"Well, what are some things in your apartment that you love?"

"Uh, my Nespresso machine... My mattress... Those are the only two things I can think of really..."

"What makes you like those?"

"Well, I guess the Nespresso machine makes me feel fancy. It provides me with a good cup of coffee. The mattress makes me feel sooo cozy and comfortable."

"Okay, so those three words are the words that you should look out for. 'Fancy.' 'Comfortable.' 'Cozy.' Look at everything in your apartment and if something doesn't make you feel any of those words, get rid of it."

That was a huge lesson for me that I still practice on my life's journey.

I continued making friends who were like-minded and also on spiritual journeys like I was. I got to enjoy Manhattan's cuisine scene. I got to explore so much of that city, which is so rich in history and culture. I learned to adjust to having to go up five flights of stairs with suitcases to move in and out, or forgetting my phone and really having to contemplate, *Do I need it today? Because I don't really feel like walking up those stairs.* Despite being from LA, where it's always so sunny, I learned to adjust to the snow and the rain and dynamic, unpredictable weather that wasn't always exactly the right kind of warm. And walking everywhere? Being able to have a meal and then walk home after? I miss it. And let me tell ya, I dropped weight, because I'd never walked so much in my life.

Living in New York was a magical time.

I can't imagine what my life would be like if I hadn't lived in Manhattan. It was such a profound, eye-opening experience, and I don't think that I'd be who I am today if I didn't take that leap. Can I be more than a Californian? Yep, I can be a New Yorker! Although I think the rule is you have to have lived there for five years before you can call yourself that. Ah well.

12

Marriage... Am I Right?

THE HUSBAND... I figure this book is the best place to tell this incredibly personal and vulnerable story. So, here's a true tale about finding *the one*, calling in *the one*, manifesting "the perfect partner." As much as this may sound like a movie script, I assure you, it isn't.

From a young age, I was one of the millions of girls who watched romance films. *Titanic. My Best Friend's Wedding. The Notebook*, which I saw three times in theaters and somehow cried more each time I watched it.

I'm also a Libra, which is the sign that revolves around the planet of Venus, the celestial body that represents love. That may play a part in why I am happiest when in a relationship. I've been in relationship after relationship because I love love and everything that has to do with it.

Since I was young, I always felt that there was this one person out there for me whom I would meet and spend my life with. I even had a sense of what he might look like. I'd always envisioned a Caucasian male with light eyes and dark hair. I would find this guy I'd concocted in my dreams. When I was out there in the world, I felt like I was always kind of looking for him, unconsciously. I always felt like I was seeking this soulmate. I thought that only if I met and fell in love with this man would I feel happy and whole. It was my belief that every relationship, even the ones I loved being in, was a checkpoint—a clue in a scavenger hunt leading me to *the* finale relationship.

I ended things with Carter because something didn't feel quite right. I didn't feel that he was *the* one. He was close, and he would've been a great partner, but he wasn't *the* guy who I knew was out there waiting for me, searching for me like I was searching for him. I moved to New York City with the intention of living, being single, being free. Which I was for a while. Then I dated Christian, the motorcycle-riding firefighter. Then Samuel. Then I told Samuel that my husband was coming so we couldn't be together.

It was Halloween night that first fall in New York. This was during the time when I was dating Christian. In fact, he and I had had a date earlier that day. We'd watched *Stand by Me* and kissed each other good night, and that was as intimate as we got. So, afterward, I got on Instagram, checking out stories and all of that. My best friend Travis had a story up, so I decided to see what he was up to without me in Los Angeles. That night, he was hanging out with these two people. One of them was Jess, a girl I knew. The other one was... well, I wasn't really sure what his name was at the time, but his Instagram account name said Raymond. This Raymond guy was petting a dog in the video, and there was something about his energy that kind of, like, touched me, stuck with me.

The day after Halloween was the day that I moved out of the apartment with the crazy landlord and into the Gramercy apartment. Once I was all settled in, I went back on Instagram on that chilly November first, looking at Raymond's page. I sat there watching his videos, laughing to myself. Smiling the whole time. There was something about this guy, whatever his name was. It said Bruce Rob on his profile, but everyone seemed to be calling him Raymond. I was sitting there like, *What is this guy's name?* It also said on his profile that he was currently living in Australia. *Damn it, that is FAR. LIKE THE FARTHEST AWAY ANYONE COULD BE FROM ME.*

After watching his videos, I thought, *You know, maybe I'll send this guy a message.* Because I felt so pulled to him. I felt that he was familiar. I felt that I had known him before. And, for the record, I'm not somebody who just sends DMs to people I don't know. So, for me to feel called to send someone a message was unique.

Upon clicking the message icon, I saw that this guy had already written me eighteen friggin' months before! My heart skipped a beat.

His message read: *You shine unlike any other human I've seen in a very long time and I'm happy to see how you're channeling your light.*

That is straight-up *MANON LINGO*! Like, that's how I speak, so it was delightfully weird and interesting to see he'd messaged me in a way that was so familiar. Like we had spent years writing and talking to each other.

Very impulsively, I wrote back: *I am having fun watching you…* And, send.

Immediately, I was like, *Why did I just send that? Oh my gosh, that's probably going to come off VERY creepy!* I beat myself up for not rereading it and thinking it over before hitting send. But everything just felt very urgent, and I felt like any time wasted would put me in danger of missing out on him or something. Like I'd just struck gold and I had to grab it immediately.

In hindsight, people say that if it's urgent, it's not spiritual. If it's meant to be, you can pause and wait. After my abnormally weird experience with this man, I'd have to say I agree. <u>Love is not something you have to grab instantly without regard. The universe moves much more slowly than we think it does. Patience, as they say, can be a virtue.</u> But, the hell with that! I found what I wanted, and I wanted it right there and then!

From that day, we messaged back and forth. Eventually, we exchanged numbers. That was around the time I ended things with Christian. Yes, after "meeting" Raymond online, before I even met him in person, I broke things off with Christian. Abruptly. And I cried my eyes out because I really liked him and I didn't want to lose him. But that's how sure of Raymond I was. I was willing to end something so great because I was so sure that I'd met my husband and I didn't want there to be any overlap between relationships at all.

That was an interesting experience, being so sure of something that I was willing to give up something else that was good. My reasoning was that I didn't want to start something new while I still had a connection or a link of any kind to another person. I didn't want any of that awkward energy. When I was younger, I used to overlap relationships, and none of it seemed to matter to me. Well, it sure mattered to their girlfriend or my boyfriend. And deep down it mattered to my soul and affected my self-esteem. It took work to forgive myself for those weak moments where I just wanted attention and didn't have the strength to say no. But now I'm really specific and have found I have to end something before I begin something else, so that I'm starting a relationship with a clean slate.

Not long into when Raymond and I started talking, he sent me a video. When I watched it, my heart dropped… I immediately felt so connected to this clip he'd sent, so I sent him a video back. He and I then promised to FaceTime that night. When his face came up on my FaceTime, it probably wasn't even a few seconds later that this thought popped into my head:

Oh, that's the man I'm going to marry.

Rob and I FaceTimed for two hours, and it was unreal. I could've cried on the phone. I was smiling ear to ear. My heart was filled. I could've told him I loved him on that first FaceTime call. I didn't. I didn't cry. I didn't say I love you. But I *COULD* have. I felt it all. I felt so deeply connected to this man whom I apparently didn't know but also felt like I knew better than anyone.

The next day we FaceTimed again, and this time, I was so overwhelmed with emotions and feelings that I *did* end up tearing up. Then he ended up tearing up too!

Are you kidding me? Is this for real? I knew it! I knew true love and this kind of fairy-tale meet-cute and descent into something incredible existed! I just knew it!

I needed to tell people that I'd hit the love jackpot. So, I texted my dad and my mom.

My mom texted me: *How was the move?*

Me: *It went well! And I met the man I'm going to marry!*

Mom: *Wow, what a day!* That response tickled me.

I texted my dad some variation of that too.

Later in the day on November 2, Raymond sent me a song—one that he loved dearly. "This is a song that I don't share with anybody," he told me, "but I feel inclined to share it with you."

Within moments of listening to this song, I thought to myself, *This song is so moving... You know what, this is our wedding song!*

And I texted that to him.

It's something that you don't say to someone after you've only been talking to them for two days.

But I felt so comfortable and free to tell my truth, and I did.

And his response? *I know it is. That's why I haven't shared it with a single soul until now...* That's what he texted me pretty much *immediately* after I hit send.

The things that were happening, the way things were playing out— it all had me like, *What the fuck is happening? Am I legit in an actual romantic movie?*

Me and Raymond began FaceTiming every day after that. One day, he happened to be visiting LA from Australia, his place of residence at the time. Of course, I no longer freaking lived there at the time. I felt bad that we wouldn't be able to be together for this chance visit. I didn't want him to go back to Australia without our meeting in person. The whole thing was consuming me because I had found my freakin' future husband.

Yes, I was claiming it already, and I was pretty much going around telling everyone that. Like, there was a party that I went to with my friend Kate, and when I walked in and she asked, "How are you?" I instantly started beaming.

"Good!" I chirped. "I met my husband."

"Wha—what do you mean? How do you know? What are you saying? What's his name?"

"Well, I don't know his name, I just know he's going to be my husband! I can't be bothered to know his name!"

And we just laughed about that.

Um, I really didn't know what his name was. He said that Bruce Henry was his birth name, so he had that name and Raymond Henry. I was like, "Okay, just pick something…" He went by Raymond because when he was younger his stepfather became a hero of his, and *his* name was Raymond. Hence his going by Ray. Are you confused? Me too!

Anyway, Raymond was in LA and he was going back to Australia, so we had planned to meet before he left. I called up my mom and told her what I was planning. Because you should always tell your parents or someone in your life when you're going to meet up in real life with someone you've only met online.

"Hey, Mom! I'm gonna have this guy who's from Perth, Australia, come stay with me for six days in New York. He happens to be in LA now and he's going to come out here before he leaves." *I've never met him before and he could be crazy, so I just wanted to let you know! K, bye!*

"Well, should I meet him first?" she said. Which made sense considering she cares about her little girl and she happens to live in LA.

"No, no. That's all right, Mom."

Then I talked to Raymond and told him the hilarious thing my mom had suggested.

"Oh, I'd love to meet your mum!"

Whoa! I thought. *He's the real deal. A true man.* Some men will date a girl for ten years and when the subject of parents comes up, they say, "*Whoa, too fast.*"

So, they met! They spent two hours together over coffee before he and I had even met in person. Yeah… That's how sure he was. That's how sure I was. There was no fear. There was no nothing. It just was what it was. And it was really crazy that it was happening. It all felt too good to be true. Waaaaay too good to be true. But that didn't stop me from jumping on board the love train, first class, full steam ahead.

Mom called me after their meeting and she went on about him being really sweet and endearing. "I have no problem with him going to stay with you, Manon." Her approval provided me with even more certainty about this dream man whom I had "finally met."

The day finally came. Raymond and I met in Madison Square Park at five fifteen in the afternoon. My heart had never raced so hard; I felt like I was going to go see the love of my life whom I had been separated from for years after World War II or something.

We came face-to-face and just melted. We held each other and we cried in each other's arms in the middle of the park!

"Where have you been?" he whispered in my ear.

I sniffled. "I've been looking everywhere for you!" I managed to say, all choked up.

It felt like two souls from a lifetime ago had found each other again in a story about reincarnation and finding your love over and over again. It was incredibly romantic. That whole week together was almost like a reconnecting and a remembering of the souls, a "soul's recognition of its counterpoint in another," like Owen Wilson said in that really deeply moving film *Wedding Crashers*.

After we'd been sitting on a park bench for over an hour, he leaned in to finally kiss me.

Gosh... took you long enough.

When he got close, we both backed away and caught our breath, thinking the same thought: *Whoa, too soon! This is too much!*

We walked his bags back up five flights of stairs to my apartment. Pretty much as soon as we set his things down, he kissed me again. And this time, it stuck. He told me he loved me, and I said it right back.

All seems a bit fast, right? But no, it didn't feel that way. It felt like this had been coming for a lifetime. It felt right. We didn't sleep together that night, although I wanted to. He was a gentleman, and waited... until the next night.

During that week together, there was a bit of an incident that happened with us outside of Eddie Bauer. It was twenty-eight degrees in Manhattan, which is beyond freezing for little ol' me, and guess who didn't have a warm enough coat? So, I bought this long, thick sausage-looking coat and I couldn't zip it up myself because it was so damn thick I could barely move. Raymond had to kneel down to assist me, so he got down on one knee and was trying to zip it.

A crowd of people began surrounding us in front of the store, gasping, going, "Where's the ring?! Where's the ring?!"

"You gotta say yes! Say yes!" one woman clamored.

Phones came out and now everyone was snapping pictures and taking videos because they thought he was proposing. To me, that was a sign for the future.

That December, we went to Montana and had a beautiful Christmas and New Year's there. Four and a half months after we met, I ended up going to Australia, where the Scotland-born Raymond had been living for eight years working in the coal mines. Yes, the same type of mines from *Zoolander* with the black lung. We traveled so I could meet his beautiful family. Meeting his mom was a gift. She felt like home.

He took me to an adorable Airbnb in a town called Margaret River. One morning we decided to go to a special beach where the river meets the sea, and he seemed a little funny. When we got there, I did what any normal person would do: I parked my towel and lay in the sun. He insisted on looking at the ocean. So we did. Then I lay back down. He then suggested we go look at the river. *What is with this guy and looking at things? We just got here! Let a girl get her tan on.*

I remember we were walking hand in hand, and he stopped and turned to me. He started saying really sweet things and it seemed like his heart was racing, working to beat right out of his chest. And this man never got nervous.

"I feel like the luckiest guy in the world to have met such a beautiful soul," he said to me. "You really are the most special person I've ever met."

OMG.

Next thing I knew, he was on one knee asking if I would marry him. He was shaking so much that he almost put the ring on the wrong hand.

"Of course I'll marry you!" I shouted, almost immediately. I couldn't have said it any faster if I'd wanted to. I can honestly say that I would've proposed to him had he not done it.

He had photographers there to capture that moment for us. Obviously, if we'd both teared up meeting in a park for the first time, you could probably guess that we both cried during the proposal— LIKE BABIES. The photos look like they are out of a movie poster. So much damn feeling!

When you know, you know. I used to hear people say that and I'd get kind of frustrated because I would think, *What if I don't know? What do I do then?* Then I finally had that "you'll just know" experience for myself.

In the early days of our engagement, Raymond stayed behind in Australia to continue working in the mines a little bit longer to make some money. He then moved across the world to New York, where we lived for six months before I finally brought him back to my home, Los Angeles.

By the way, Raymond's birthday happens to be the same exact day that my parents got married in Hawaii. To the year! That was a mother-effin' sign from the universe that this guy was born for me—a sign that made me feel like this was the right move.

We shouted our story from the rooftops and all over social media. Anyone and everyone in my life confirmed that he was in fact PERFECT for me. We just fit. When we would go out to events, somehow, we couldn't even help but dance the exact same way. Everything we did was in sync. Not long after, my dad revealed to me that Raymond had asked him for my hand in marriage and that he'd made a promise to my father to take care of me, support me, and cherish my heart forever.

Cut to: Our beautiful wedding... Ugh, it was absolutely stunning. I did a bridal campaign where I was gifted three gorgeous wedding dresses. I wore all three that day because I couldn't decide which one I loved more. We were fortunate enough to get many of the big elements for free. The cake bakers, DJs, florists, videographers, and photographers were all happy to provide their services in exchange for shout-outs on my page. Lucky me. Having a following really comes in handy when you don't have $50K lying around for a one-day event. But I had dreamed of this day since I was a little girl, so even if I had spent that, it would have been worth it! My dad crushed it by paying for the rest, which wasn't cheap. Thank you for the beautiful day, Dad.

Everything just worked out perfectly, like the universe or some higher power was showering us with gifts for being on the right path with each other. Ironically, the very talented singer Kina Grannis, who sang "Can't Help Falling in Love" in the movie *Crazy Rich Asians,* sang the *same song* at our wedding. You know, the song with the bit about fools rushing in? Well, my use of the word "ironically" will become clear in a few pages.

Wait for it...

Days before the wedding of our dreams, I purchased my first home. I bought it for us so we could spend the rest of our days together making babies and living a blissful life. We got to have our rehearsal dinner in the new house, where our families could spend time getting to know one another. We all sat around, and then, one by one, everyone shared funny stories about the bride and groom.

About a month after the wedding, I got the wedding photos. Holy moly, were they stunning. Each photo was better than the last. If you work at a magazine and you need wedding photos, please hit me up. As I looked at the photos with glee, my bestie/bridesman Travis called me up. I had not a hint, not a clue, that a bomb was going to go off.

13

The Bomb Drops

"HEY, WHAT ARE you doing?" Travis asked, nervousness in his voice.

"I got the wedding photos! I'm just looking through them now."

"Nice, nice… Listen, can we meet up for a coffee, Manon?"

"Um… sure. Why don't you come over and look at the wedding photos?"

"I'd prefer it if you'd come out with me and Cathy," he said solemnly. Cathy is his girlfriend.

Okay, that's weird… Maybe they're surprising me with something…

So, they took me to a coffee shop and sat down across from me. Travis and Cathy reached over and grabbed my arm, looking at me with concern and sadness. The whole situation felt heavy. I instinctively knew something horrible was coming my way.

Travis took a deep breath, then let it out slowly. "What I'm about to tell you isn't going to be easy to hear… " he said.

My heart dropped. My whole body started tingling, then shaking. The feeling that rushed over me was unlike anything I've ever felt. Automatically, fear dropped in and consumed me. *Are they going to tell me that Raymond died… ? What's going on!?* Like, it was just so dramatic. It was *sooo* dramatic.

"Tell me!" I said, panicked. "What's—what's going on?" I stuttered.

Travis looked at me with a broken heart; I could see the pain he felt coming from his heart through his eyes. "So… this girl messaged me saying, '*I'm sending you this message because Manon's really going to need a friend right now. Her husband has been sending me inappropriate messages for a few weeks now and I have screenshots to prove it.*'"

Travis slowly turned his phone to where I could see it. The messages that I saw were... *highly* sexual in nature. First texts, then photos, then videos. WTF was happening? I couldn't breathe at this point. I was so confused. Then I saw more: he was naked, and then he was saying things about ME—talking smack about me! He said things along the lines of, "Manon's boring. She's not sexy. I'm about to blow up on the RED CARPET and I want YOU by my side!"

What in the actual fuck...

He was saying this to a stranger. It was so fucked up... *so* fucked up! I *literally* felt like my whole world had just flipped upside down—exploded from an asteroid strike... I—I—I... I couldn't believe it. There was no way! But I had to believe it because I saw the screenshots and videos. Not only did he write mean things about me, he told her he loved her and that they had been together in past lives. A lot of the things he said to me, he'd said to her, a complete stranger. The words that I had held so dear, which I'd thought were just for me, were now being given to her—not to mention a few other women, as I'd find out later.

This news was so excruciating and confusing, because to my face, he treated me like a queen. I'd chosen him and kept falling more in love with him because of his kindness to others, his warm heart, his presence, the face he made when I sang, the face he made when he cried. The way he held space for me when I cried. He was always carrying my bags and being of service to anyone and everybody. He was kind to animals. He was always there for me. So, to think of his being always there but then sneaking off to the bathroom and touching himself in the shower with a stranger, saying "I love you" to her, was sooo creepy and scary that it really freaked me the hell out. He called her his TRUE QUEEN. I mean... get the fuck out of here. It made me feel like I did not know who I'd married. Well, I didn't. I was so blindsided, so embarrassed, so confused about how this could have happened. And for this to happen so soon after our wedding? It was like being stabbed in the heart, repeatedly.

The good news is, I had done enough spiritual growth before this happened not to jump off a bridge. I remembered what I had learned about not taking things personally. But come on… this?! *Nope, Manon, this is not about you,* I reminded myself. Because it wasn't. It had everything to do with him, his insecurities and his need for attention and approval. So, luckily, I didn't think, *Wait, what? I'm not sexy? What? I'm boring?* Because I know deep down none of that's true. He had to make me small so he could feel bigger.

Either way, it definitely was a huge letdown. And he broke a lot of people's hearts, including mine, my parents', and my friends'. And then there was his poor family, who had just spent all of their savings to fly across the world to be at the wedding.

An hour after I heard this news, I confronted him about it. He quickly admitted to the whole thing. He got on his knees and apologized. "What can I do to make this right?" he groveled. "I will do anything…"

For the next forty-eight hours, I proceeded to hold him while he sobbed his eyes out. I saged him. I showered him. It was almost like he had never dealt with anything in his life and it all just came rushing out. I saw him as a little boy in pain and I was able to hold the space for him. How the eff did I not punch him in the face? NO FREAKIN' CLUE! God stepped in, and I was able to see him as a flawed human being who hated himself.

Everyone has demons from their past. No matter how big or small they are, if we don't deal with them, they'll come out somehow. I don't think he'd ever really dealt with his past before, so it all finally hit him at once. And, again, because I had done some healing work leading up to this point, I didn't scream, I didn't kick, I didn't throw shit. I think I scare myself when I get too angry. In later months, I screamed like I had never screamed before, because he told me to. "Let it out, give it to me," he said. "I deserve it. This is mine to deal with, nobody else's."

I thank him for that. Bottling up my anger was the last thing I wanted to do, because when I do that, it ends up manifesting internally, giving me an upset tummy. I used to think my anger was ugly, but, apparently, we could use more sacred rage in our lives. My message to you is: let it out! Throw that tantrum, add a little playfulness to it, fall to the ground. Express yourself! Your partner can handle it. And if they can't… well, find a new one. But please make sure you give them a warning before giving in to your feelings. I think we could all feel a little more.

Two days later, I told Raymond to move out. That was excruciating for me but necessary for my personal well-being. It was a powerful exercise in setting boundaries. And then I made another decision. Because we were married, I decided not to walk away immediately. There were times that I had messed up in my life when I was given the chance to better myself. I knew people had the capacity to change, and I wanted to give him an honest opportunity to work on his issues. After all, we had the kind of story that movies are made of. Maybe our movie could have a final act, one of joyous redemption.

We went to counseling for three months, and that helped me to forgive him. I hope it helped him to forgive himself. Not just for betraying me, but for betraying himself. I didn't condone what he did, but I was able to forgive. As Marianne Williamson once said, "Until we have seen someone's darkness, we don't really know who they are. Until we have forgiven someone's darkness, we don't really know what love is." It was an exceptional healing process that deepened my security with myself and helped me realize that *hurt people hurt people*. A person who wasn't in pain couldn't have done what he'd done. His text-capades demonstrated how much actual pain he was in that I didn't know about. Unfortunately, now I have this sex-tape of his running in my brain that I'd really, really like to delete from my memory… Yikes!

Nevertheless, witnessing what he had done showed me that there was nothing I could've done to alter his behavior. It was clear that if he hadn't hurt me, he would've eventually hurt somebody else. Instead of reprimanding him, I sought to find love and compassion for the parts of him that hurt, which has, astonishingly, only made me feel stronger.

That "Shining Prince" morphing into the "Prince of Darkness" experience was the *BIGGEST* heartbreak I've ever had. It was the most profound blindside of my entire life so far.

Take a breath. I need it. You MAY need it.

Where do we stand today? We decided to be nothing more than friends and we are currently going through a divorce. My trust had been pulverized, and in order for him to move forward with me, he would have to want to fundamentally alter his pain. I wasn't seeing the changes I needed to see to keep going. I didn't have the energy to keep hoping for something that might never come. I didn't want to live my life always looking over my shoulder at who he was texting. Maybe if we were in a long-term relationship with a family, I would consider spending more time working on it. But I ain't God. I can't change others. I can only change me and my own behavior.

So we're not in a romantic relationship anymore. I also don't believe that when you separate from someone, it means you can never talk again. I think it's possible, in this world we live in, to grieve the end of a relationship with your ex, so long as there wasn't horrendous physical and/or mental abuse. Despite this terrible betrayal, I can still grieve the loss of him with him, and vice versa. I'm not somebody who wants to hold on to that anger. I want to let it go. And because I'm not participating in a romantic relationship with him, that is me taking care of myself.

Ultimately, I don't want to build on something that's broken. Because trust is so important. And I didn't realize how powerful trust is until this happened. It's kind of the root of everything working smoothly. If I don't trust my partner, my body closes up and then I'm unable to be intimate with them. So much of communication is nonverbal. If you can't feel open to and trusting of your partner, what's left?

Even though we did try to make it work, it was just too early in the relationship to have that deep of a betrayal; I don't think our love was enough to survive it. No one's is.

I gave it my all before I met him, during our time together, and after finding out what happened. Now I find myself sending Raymond love often. And I pray for him. That's my part. And that's what makes me feel better. So, that's that.

There is the occasional moment when I cry and get angry and feel scared and want to close up. But that lasts only a few minutes. I don't try to run from those feelings. I let them come and go.

In the months after I received that wound to my heart, every part of me wanted to close off and say, *"Screw this! Screw relationships!"* Every fiber of my being wanted to get angry and never dabble in partnership again.

When I sat across from my therapist, surrounded by snotty tissues, and told him I never wanted to feel like this again, he said, "Stay open. Be willing to get shot in the heart a hundred times but still reveal that love, because the alternative is, what? To live with a closed heart? That's no way to live at all. Be willing to be a target for love."

It would be such a shame for me to close my heart because of another man's pain. It wouldn't be fair to the young Manon who had hopes and dreams of finding that love she believed in her core was out there.

Sure, I married the man of my dreams, I bought a house, I expected to have kids with this man, and… now we're just friends. Maybe it didn't go as planned. Or maybe it did? There's a higher power at work in our lives, so maybe that was just a road sign telling me where to go next in life.

One thing is clear: I feel stronger than ever now. I feel like a warrior. I feel like I can get through anything now. Not to mention, a month after I found out about all of this, I got a call from a friend who had just dealt with something really similar. Had I not gone through that experience, I wouldn't have been able to be of service to her and help guide her through this part of her journey with her boyfriend, whom she'd caught waking up in *their* bed with his ex. Jeez. Dudes! Just let her know you're scared and don't want to be committed to just one lady. She will be pissy in the moment but she'll ultimately respect your honesty.

Being deceived in that way was never something I thought I'd have to deal with. I never really understood the pain of people I knew who had been cheated on. But I believe that my pain and my experience was worth going through if it means I can help even just *one* person. And that's why I am sharing this story here. I didn't even plan on sharing this with the public. It's not for a pity party or a selling point. This is me sharing a vulnerable slice with the world in hopes of reaching as many people as I can who might find themselves in a similar situation.

This whole chapter of heartache was kind of a lesson of forgiveness, because most of the people in my life don't understand how or why I could even talk to a man who told me he loved me and then spewed such foul crap about me and did what he did. I do know that everybody deserves forgiveness and, at times, even a second chance. And the more we can expand our hearts and forgive, the more healing takes place. But also know when to walk away. That comes in handy.

14

Hello Again, Samuel...

SAMUEL, THE GUY who'd created a line of blue-light-blocking glasses, made a profound difference in my life, so I want to double back a bit to speak on how he affected my personal growth.

The change he manifested in me comes from his communication style. He's actually popped back up several times over the last few years. In a platonic capacity, of course. There was one more interesting experience between him and me (and Raymond) that is worth sharing because I think it speaks volumes about how to resolve complicated situations that can crop up while you're in a relationship.

In most situations, when a man and a woman are together and there's a third party who comes in, things can get chaotic and dramatic. Arguments can break out, and violence may arise. All of that is because of the perceived "ownership" that can come with some relationships and the threat to a commitment and a partnership.

With that said, Samuel would show up in town every now and then, and we'd grab a meal or a coffee. I felt we shared a really strong connection. He challenged my mind, and I became curious about his success. Our connection was of a friendly nature, so I felt that it didn't need to completely die out. I figured, *Okay, we'll stay friends.*

Maybe a little less than a year after Raymond and I met, while I was living in New York, I traveled back to LA for a job. Raymond stayed in New York at our place. Samuel was visiting LA, so he asked to get together for an early dinner in Santa Monica, where I happened to be at that time. I thought, *Sure, why not.*

At the restaurant, he ordered two ginger beers and was buzzing from the sugar. Neither of us were drinkers, so we were hyper-present. He sat across from me with an interesting look on his face. It was a knowing look that felt full of curiosity. After a brief pause, he began telling me that he'd consulted with his relationship coach, his intimacy coach, and friends that he trusted, asking their advice on whether or not he should let me know of his feelings for me.

OMG. I did not see that comin'!

"They all told me that it's okay for me to let you know that I *do* have romantic feelings for you, as you're not married yet," he confessed. "I'm not asking anything from you, but what I am letting you know is what I can provide you. I can provide you with travel. I can pay for you if you don't want to work, though I know that you like to work. I would be present with you and give great communication and deep intimacy. This is what I'm offering you." Basically, he presented a brochure of what he would provide me in a relationship.

WHOA, DUDE! I just started my salad! But tell me more…

I sat across from him in silence, kind of blown away by his proposal because he wasn't making any advances; he wasn't being disrespectful or crossing any suggestive or physical lines. Samuel was just sharing his own feelings, laying his cards out on the table. He wasn't pretending to be my friend. He was being authentic and honest. He was doing it for himself. Taking care of his own heart, I suppose.

After that conversation, we walked to the car and I said, "Maybe it's worth me sharing this again, but I *do* want you to know that I *do* love the man that I'm engaged to."

"That's good for me to hear. Would you be open to a romantic relationship with me?"

"I'm in a relationship… " I declared.

"Well, would he be open to you having another relationship?"

Eyes wide and nervously smiling with my jaw hanging, my best answer at the time was, "I don't know!"

"Okay. Well, I look forward to hearing from you."

That whole situation had me feeling like a deer in headlights. *Um, what? What a weird… what are you talking about? What are you saying? Is that a thing people do? Am I weird for being weirded out?!*

Then a pang of guilt and remorse overcame me. *Am I so dumb and oblivious that I didn't see this coming? Did I do something wrong here? I gotta talk to my fiancé!*

Keeping that to myself was out of the question. Raymond hadn't displayed any jealousy up until this point, so I figured he wouldn't flip out. He's a *very* understanding man and had held space beautifully for me in times where I criticized myself. One of the things I love about him is his ability to be understanding. After saying goodbye to Samuel, I immediately called Raymond and told him everything.

He didn't love it. Duh. In fact, he was pretty threatened by it. What he could've done was gone and kicked Samuel's ass and said, "Ay! Fuck you!" Apparently, what he did instead was reach out to Samuel on Instagram and ask to have a phone call. And they did. The Scotsman and the Australian had a civil phone call. Raymond shared with Samuel his feelings about what Samuel had done. Samuel shared his. *They* shared feelings! Two grown men talking it out?!

The phone call ended with Samuel's saying, "Hey, Raymond, if you need any sort of advice on your citizenship stuff, let me know, because I've been through it."

CLICK.

Cut to me scratching my head.

After that, nothing ever arose out of that situation again, because it had all been dealt with. Everyone had expressed their feelings easily and there was no tension. I was honest. I didn't lie. I didn't hide anything. I shared what happened freely, without delay. Samuel shared his feelings for me. Raymond shared his feelings with Samuel. Samuel held the space for Raymond, and they both shared their feelings with me.

That whole situation of another man's coming into the mix of my engagement could've been a catastrophe. But it ended up not being detrimental to my relationship because of the honesty that everyone exhibited. Unfortunately, that kind of honesty is rare; most people mask their vulnerabilities and their concerns. No movie could ever be made from the whole me, Samuel, and Raymond thing, because movies need drama, and there really wasn't much drama. What little drama there was came and went within forty-eight hours.

This is a story that I've told close friends before, but I wanted to share this here to show what's possible in life when you communicate openly, let people be heard, and open the floor to unfiltered expressions of emotion. Everyone can heal and grow more quickly without any hindrances and secrets, or lying. Which leads me to my next chapter...

15

Things That Happen in LA: Dating a Celebrity

IT WAS 2013, right before I took off on Vine. I went to a twelve-step meeting because I had just gotten through my first year of sobriety and I was asked to speak a lot. In the program, they usually have someone speak for ten to fifteen minutes at each meeting, then everyone else gets to share their experience for three minutes or so. It's amazing, because there's no one person who runs the meetings; they're run by the group as a whole. Without an ultimate authority or a hierarchy, the only power present is the power of support and community.

On this particular night, I was asked to speak at this Hollywood meeting at 10:00 P.M. I spent my ten minutes or so talking about my past and the importance of surrendering to my circumstances, and as I scanned the faces before me, I noticed a familiar one.

OH! I recognize him! He was in a few movies that I love!

Given this man was in the program, for the sake of preserving his anonymity, I'll go ahead and call him by a deceased celebrity's name. Let's go with Cary Grant. Cary was and still is a big-time celebrity whom I had been crushing on for quite some time by this point.

So, when I noticed him, I had to really focus on keeping it together and not let my excitement show on my face. *This is not my primary purpose. My purpose is to share my story, not to obsess about the guy I have a crush on in the meeting,* I told myself.

After the meeting, he came up to me and said, "Hey! I really enjoyed what you shared tonight." He said that he had ninety days sober, so I really had to put my fangirl away to be of service to him. I'm generally pretty good at shifting gears when I know my goal is to listen and be present for someone. Cary went on to say that he was also a writer and he felt like he wasn't going to be able to write anymore because he was sober.

I totally related to him, so I said, "Listen, I absolutely get it. I thought that I wasn't going to be funny anymore when I stopped drinking, but it wasn't until I was six months sober that I even thought about doing stand-up. For artists who get sober, it's a common fear that we won't be able to be creative if we're not, you know, drinking or getting high or whatever it is. It'll pass."

"Thank you for saying that. I really needed to hear that."

"You're welcome... Hey, you know what? You should come to the meetings that I go to in the Valley."

He smiled. "Okay, cool. Yeah, maybe I'll check it out."

When I met him, I also met the actress he was there with; let's call her Audrey Hepburn. After Cary Grant walked away, I talked with her for a bit and got some insight into his relationship status. Audrey said that she had a mini-crush on him too but that nothing had ever happened between them because she didn't date people in the program. That definitely got me excited. *Okay, they're not together*, I thought. *Even though they're hanging out, they're not together. So maybe there's a chance for me, because I feel a very strong pull.*

Two days later, as I was walking up to my usual meeting, I saw him outside, sitting on the bench. And I lit up! I was so excited that he had come, because we'd gotten along really well when we met. I trotted on over to him, arms out and flapping like I was a vulture or something, like a weirdo... I don't know why I did that.

Thankfully, he stood up and laughed at my silly-ass approach. Then I gave him a big hug. There was definitely a spark.

Sometime later, I was driving in Hollywood with Amy and I got a text from Audrey Hepburn. Her text said: *Hey, my friend Cary Grant wants your number because he wants to set you up with his friend. Can I give him your number?*

Reading that made me scream, "Oh my God! Oh my God!" I was just ecstatic, because I was thinking, *He doesn't want to set me up. No guy's thinking about setting his boy up. He wants my number to take me out! That's what's really up here.*

Not long after I told Audrey to give him my number, he texted me: *Hey, this is Cary Grant. I'd like to take you out with my friend Paul Newman. Are you available this weekend?*

The guy I'm referring to as Paul Newman was another A-list actor. He was hilarious. My response to that: *What? Absolutely!*

So, a few days later, there I was. I was out in Los Feliz at the Dresden on a double date with Cary freaking Grant and Paul damn Newman, having an unbelievably great night. Cary's date was Audrey. I noticed myself feel a tinge of envy that she was with him instead of me. But Paul Newman and I clicked very well. Cary was really in awe of how quickly we connected.

"It feels like you guys have known each other forever," Cary told me.

I was confused because I wanted to date Cary and I thought he'd felt the same spark I had the last time we were together. I didn't understand why he would set me up with Paul Newman. *Oh,* I thought, *maybe he did just want to set me up.*

At the end of the night, Paul Newman and I exchanged numbers.

Three weeks later, I was filming a really low-budget feature film called *Welcome to Forever* up in Big Bear with a bunch of friends. (And when I say "low-budget," I mean I did it for free.)

It was me, my friend Amy, and a few other people, and we basically did it for fun. We were shooting in and around a cabin for seven days. I played a lesbian, which was a first for me. How was it, you might ask?

It was, uh… kind of exciting. I like doing things that I'm uncomfortable with and not used to. There was this scene in a Jacuzzi where my character made a move on a lovely young lady with long brown hair and very soft skin. My character was unsure of her character's feelings, so I had to kiss her, then back away, going, "Oh my God, I'm sorry!" The funny thing is, when I watch that scene back, I think I actually do sound a little bit like Kristen Stewart because I was all stumbly with my words. I can see why I was compared to her.

So, anyway, I prepped myself for this scene and then we filmed it. Her lips were a lot softer than I was used to. I was like, *Oh my gawd, is this what it's like?* I kissed a girl. And I liked it. A lot. But not enough to shift my sexuality.

Not only was I a lesbian in this film, but I had to also play drunk, which was interesting being that I was a year sober. I don't love playing drunk. I don't think people should ever play drunk unless they're *actually* drunk. It looks DUMB! It reads to me as inauthentic, which takes me out of the scene. If I ever land a movie role that requires me to act drunk, I will break my damn sobriety just to make sure that the scene is authentic! JK…

While I was up there filming this movie, Paul Newman was texting me. But so was Cary Grant… And Cary Grant started sending me *very* flirtatious texts. That was kind of a problem for me, because clearly there was something going on between him and Audrey Hepburn. So I was like, *No! This sucks! I wanted to date Cary Grant! Yet, he's texting me these messages that are flirtatious in nature…*

At one point, I just texted him something like: *Wait, aren't you dating Audrey Hepburn?*

Cary Grant: *Yeah… She probably wouldn't be thrilled that I'm texting you. So we'll keep it friendly.*

Me: *Okay. Sounds good!*

A couple days went by and we continued texting each other. He sent me a selfie. I sent him one back. They were really cute. Nothing dirty. But then he kind of crossed the line and said: *I want you to come over and watch a movie with me.*

I was twenty-four years old and there was a huge celebrity texting me to come spend time with him. Of course I wanted to say yes! But I had set some standards for myself at this point.

1. I didn't want to be involved with anyone who was in any sort of relationship with another girl while he was flirting with me and asking me to spend time with him.

2. I was not just going to go to a guy's house. Like, take me out to dinner and court me!

3. I also didn't love that he was only three months sober. That's like dating someone who is just learning to walk again. I never want to feel like I'm taking advantage of anyone.

So, that's basically what I let him know.

"That's fine," he said in response. "We'll be friends. We'll go to a friendly lunch at some point."

I was so proud of myself that I'd set these standards and maintained these boundaries. And I was so glad that he was okay with them.

I went to the Groundlings class I was taking at the time, and I remember being so stoked that I was flirting with this celebrity, because I'd idolized celebrities since I was a little girl growing up in LA and I aspired to be a movie star myself. I thought that they were bigger and better than us "normal" people. That's probably because they literally were big on the screen in these bright, vivid colors, so in my unconscious mind, they loomed so large to me! Weird, right? That's why they make such a big impression on us. From a neurological perspective, it's because of how big they literally appear to us on-screen versus how we see ourselves in our unconscious mind. If we see a big, bright, larger-than-life moving picture of ANY human, we are more likely to respond to them as if they have some superpower when we see them in person.

If you want to change things as they appear in the unconscious mind, you have to visualize them in your mind as black and white and make them very small. Then they cannot have such a strong effect on you and your mind, and in turn your nervous system. Since this chapter of my life, I've learned to do that with celebrities, and they're not a big deal to me anymore. I've made them smaller—right sized—in my brain, so we're all equal. I remind myself that we're all connected. It's actually helped my anxiety level when I meet other celebrities.

But at the time, I was not big on Vine yet, so this was a huge thing that was happening for me. And I tried to keep my cool. I remember going to a film the next day. I felt lonely. I remember driving, looking at the moon, and having the thought, *You only live once. He's inviting you over again. This opportunity may never come back.*

Then another thought followed. *I wanna get to know him! I like him! I'm going to follow my heart!* And I remember swerving into a right turn and saying, "I'm going to his house!"

Cary lived in West Hollywood in this beautiful, massive house with a Vespa in the driveway. I felt an immediate pull to hop on that thing with him and ride into the sunset. *This guy seems pretty great*, I thought, staring at it all in awe.

Cary greeted me at the door and wrapped those long arms around me. I remember feeling so nervous at that moment, unsure of what the night would bring. I walked in and noticed he had a whole library of all these incredible books and a really clean house with an amazing backyard, and I thought, *Man, this guy is living the dream.* You know, besides the fact that he was ninety days sober and probably got there because he maybe burned his life to the ground. We never know why people get sober. But if there's one thing I've learned on my journey, it's that people don't get sober by accident. They don't check out twelve-step meetings because they're curious. It's the last house on the block, and they have no other place to turn to for help.

I find that pain is the touchstone of spiritual growth for people. No one really decides to change unless they have to—unless they're fed up with how they have been living. We don't realize we can either learn through pain or learn through joy. Most people unfortunately learn through pain until they have to change. I mean, who really just up and changes who they are when they're feeling okay? No one, really. They change because they have no other way.

Cary and I watched a movie together. Midway through, he began putting the moves on me. We had a nice make-out sesh and did some other fun things.

After all the tonsil hockey, he went outside to go smoke a cigarette, and I sat on the couch alone with my thoughts. *Oh my God, is this going to be my next relationship!? I'm in HEAVEN right now!*

When he came back from his smoke break, we cuddled, which wasn't as pleasant as I would've liked it to be because I hate cigarette smoke. It's disgusting and a huge turnoff for me because I'm allergic. But for him? I overrode that. *Well, it doesn't matter. This is Cary Grant, after all.*

"Would you like to spend the night?" he asked softly.

In my mind, I was thinking, *No! I can be intimate but not that intimate!*

As I mulled over how I should respond, Amy called and said that she was locked out of the house. That was my out.

"I gotta go! My roommate is locked out!"

I remember driving away feeling so full, like, *Oh my gawd, I didn't even need to sleep over. I feel so strong right now. He wanted more and I didn't. And I'm out of here!*

Despite feeling amazing about the evening we shared together, I also felt bad about it. I mean, he and Audrey weren't, like, *exclusive* or anything, but they were definitely dating, and I knew her—not well, but still, it sat uncomfortably in me.

That tinge of guilt crept back up when he texted me a few days later asking if I'd like to hang out again. *I think it's best that we're just friends because you're seeing this other girl and I don't feel good about that.* That's what I texted him. It was hard.

That following Monday, he hit me with this: *Hey, just so you know, I broke it off with Audrey.*

I should've taken that as a sign, like, *Oh, he did that to pursue things with me.* But I didn't. Maybe I was scared. Maybe I was afraid that if he could break things off with her like that, he could do the same to me. That fear prompted me to respond with: *Can we stay friends?*

Two weeks later, I went back on the whole "let's be friends" thing. I went to his house and then we did sleep together. And it was incredible. It felt amazing. The whole night was full of laughs and play. Then, at the end of the night, he asked me to spend the night again. I said no and I left again, feeling so empowered. I imagine he took that as a hint that I didn't want to get close to him. Or maybe he didn't. Who knows? I don't, because shortly after we slept together, he left town to film a movie and then we lost touch for a while.

When he returned from filming, he invited me to come see him. Given that I had been thinking about him on and off during the time that he was away and wondering if I'd ever see him again, it goes without saying that I was beyond excited that he wanted to see me so soon after coming home.

Cary Grant had a new house up north, where he invited me to spend the night with him. He took me out to dinner, he kissed me on the street, he took me for an amazing meal at the best restaurant in town, and then we shared a milkshake after. When I was on the way back to the table from the bathroom, he stared at me, smiling.

I smiled back. "What?"

"You have such a presence about you. You have such power and beauty."

He's smitten, and so am I.

After that, we went back to his place and got it on again. We lay there afterward and he poked me (with his finger) and said all these cute little things that only made me like him more.

The next morning, he took me to breakfast. Then he took me around and introduced me to some friendly people in his neighborhood. *He must really like me*, I thought. I drove away from his place that night feeling so empowered and giddy.

Cary Grant's life got busy after we spent those twenty-four hours together, so there was a long spell where I didn't hear from him. Jimmy Fallon beckoned. The promo tour for his new movie demanded his presence.

Personally, what I expect from someone I'm dating is for them to call or check in from time to time. Unfortunately, what I got from Cary was infrequent contact. I require more connection and attention from a man that I'm sharing my mind, body, and soul with, even in the face of a hectic lifestyle, because I feel like there is always time that can be made for people you truly care for. That said, I made his lack of contact out to mean that he didn't care about me—that he really wasn't into me like I was into him.

At one point, I sat down with my sponsor to vent about how hard his being unavailable was for me.

"Is this your ideal relationship?" she asked.

Ultimately, I decided that it wasn't. I mean, it was when we were together, because he was amazing, we always had fun, and he always made me laugh. But then when we were apart, I had too much time to guess about what he might be thinking.

It got to the point where I just flat-out texted him to see if he could be in touch more.

Cary texted me something like: *I'm unavailable for phone calls but I can text.*

Me: *I mean, that's not good enough for me.*

It was clear that if I was going to be with him, I had to shrink in order to match him. Or he had to stretch in order to match me. Either way, one of us was going to have to shift. Shrinking for someone else was out of the question. I wanted to be expansive. I wanted to be more connected. I wanted to grow.

Months later, following my rise on Vine, I ended up being on this TBS show called *Funniest Wins*, hosted by Marlon Wayans. It was Vine stars and internet sensations going up against career comedians to see who'd come out on top. Jason Nash and Ryan Doon were on there with me. Tiffany Haddish was also on the show, along with a few other hilarious comedians. The competitions were various forms of comedy, like stand-up challenges, *SNL* Lonely Island–style music videos, short sketches, pranks, etc.

Being on *Funniest Wins* was an intense, nerve-wracking, beautiful experience. We were sequestered in a DoubleTree hotel downtown across from some prison for a month. That meant we couldn't see family or friends or anyone like that the entire time.

I wasn't super thrilled about my time on the show. It wasn't because I wasn't doing well, because I was. I was judging the show on the fact that it was only going to be on TBS instead of Fox or whatever. And I was also a little disappointed that I was on a competition show rather than a sitcom. One night, I talked to Cary Grant on the phone about how I was feeling. Cary had been on a hit sitcom, so he shared with me the insight he'd gotten from that experience, and he was incredibly helpful.

"I missed the experience of being on the show because I was so focused on what other people were doing that was better than what I was doing. I regret comparing and despairing instead of appreciating every moment that I was on that show. So don't go missing the experience like I did. Be present and trust that you're in the right place."

Wow, I thought. *I was missing the miracle of the gifts that are being given to me in this moment because I'm in too much fear.*

Cary went on to explain this analogy that has stuck with me ever since. It was about the ocean (life) and swimming toward a destination. Sometimes there's a place you're swimming to that you think you really need to get to, but the waves work against you, leaving you to struggle against the current until you tire yourself out. The thing is, the ocean wants you to go in the direction in which the waves are trying to carry you, so you can get to this other spot that's *far* better than what you're fighting to get to. So, only by relaxing and taking it easy and chilling can you float to where you're supposed to be, a *much* more beautiful place in life.

My limited brain only sees so much, a sliver of space between me and the path before me leading to the goal I'm working toward. But the Universe sees *way* more and knows what's better for me. And if I just relax, I'll enjoy the ride more and I'll get to where I'm supposed to be without suffering.

That analogy he shared changed my perspective forever, and I appreciate him so very much for sharing that with me. Maybe that single bit of wisdom that he gifted me was the whole reason we met in the first place. Because I've been blessed enough to pass along that message to hundreds and hundreds of people at this point. And hopefully now I can share it with thousands after putting it into this book.

Comparing and despairing about being on *Funniest Wins* was behind me, but I still had this other thing eating away at me: fear. There were times on the show when I was in so much fear that they were going to try to make me look bad because it was "reality TV," which is known for being anything but real. Reality depended on the perception the producers created through editing. I was worrying so much about how they might make me look that I wasn't taking in the opportunity as the gift that it was. *I was chosen over someone who probably would've killed for this opportunity. How can I keep being of service?*

I lost my way a little bit, functioning from fear rather than through my love of all things comedy, because I felt so out of control. So powerless. I experienced such intense fear that I got sick afterward with a monthlong bout of ulcerative colitis. The day I got eliminated kicked off over thirty days of pretty horrendous health issues brought on from stress that *I* created for no reason.

During this time of battling my ulcerative colitis flare-up, Cary Grant invited me back up north again to stay with him as a friend in his guesthouse. The thing is, I wasn't a cute sick. I wasn't like, *"Yeah, I'm cute, I have a cold, you can come take care of me and feed me soup!"* It was like, *"I'm in the bathroom all day, sick… so…"*

You know, I think the universe was protecting me, because, again, I'd have had to shrink if I was going to be with this person. Not only that, but I was going to be on the arm of a celebrity when I wanted to be the star of my life. I don't want to feel second best to someone.

On the Fourth of July, we'd gone to a celebration with fireworks at a high school. Every time one of my Vine followers recognized me, I would look back at Cary, smirking. He just laughed and went on about how funny it was that he was an actual celebrity and not getting recognized while I was. I mean, that was because of demographics, but it still gave my ego a boost that I needed at the time and kind of reminded me that I wanted to achieve success and stardom on my own instead of being recognized as a celebrity's girlfriend. I want to impact the world with light and love of my own accord.

After he said he was only free for texting, I started thumbing another text to him: *I don't know if this is working out. I just kinda wanna be friends…*

Following that conversation, I may have shot myself in the foot. He had let me know that his sister was eleven days sober and he'd invited her to a meeting. That day, Cary's sister asked me to sponsor her. Instead of saying, *"Hey, no, I have a crush on your brother so it's probably not a good idea,"* I said, "Sure, I'll sponsor you!"

Once I became her sponsor, Cary Grant stopped pursuing me once and for all. And rightly so, because he cared about his sister. Or maybe not; maybe I was just a booty call.

When I asked my sponsor what I should do about the whole situation, she told me, "You know, your primary purpose is to stay sober and to help another alcoholic."

With that said, I put helping her in front of my feelings for him. And I got my wish. He and I were just friends.

I'm sure that there's a reason for that.

A few months later, I found out he had a new girlfriend. And that was just the closure I needed to finally move on. *If he wanted you, he would've claimed you. He would've taken you out*, I thought. *If someone wants you, they will make it known. There's nothing that would keep them from you.*

Occasionally, Cary and I will still check in with each other to see how we're doing. Sometimes I see that he watches my Snapchat stories. But my obsession with him has been removed, I think because of experiences that the universe provided for me, like my being sick when he wanted to see me, and his sister coming in and requiring me to be of service to her, which took my focus away from him.

Speaking of his sister, I sponsored her for a year and she's still sober to this day. As of 2020, that's six years of sobriety! She is a wonderful, beautiful human being whom I wouldn't have had the pleasure of getting to know had I not met him. I didn't know why he was brought into my life. I thought it was to teach me how to shift my perspective in a way that allows me to go with the flow and to be grateful for every opportunity that I get. But maybe it was to help his sister. Maybe both.

Dating Cary Grant around the time I started getting kind of recognized helped me to see us all as one, to see us all as connected. Now I approach all people as if I know them, even if they are celebrities. Like the time I saw Steve Carell outside of Papyrus, the stationery store.

"Steve!" I called out like I hadn't seen him in months.

"Hey!" he said with a curious smile, eyes searching me as his brain worked to put a name to my face.

"Oh, I don't actually know you… I'm just a fan, and I think you're wonderful!"

I engaged him with the energy of feeling like I already knew him because I don't think anyone is better than me and I don't think anyone is worse. I think we're all the same, which is important for all of us to remember. In twelve-step, they talk about being "right sized." Making the ego right sized. The ego is what makes us feel separate when we should be connecting through that which binds us all: love. Love is God reminding me that we're all one, we're all on this planet together, and my ego is the thing that makes me want to feel not part of—it makes me want to feel better than someone or less than someone.

The ego sometimes is run by fear. It wants to protect itself and it's doing the best it can. But, ultimately, it's what causes a lot of the grief and frustration and pain in life. I know it has in my life. When I remember that love is all there is, and that either God is everything or God is nothing, then I'm in peace and filled with love and joy and gratitude. Either I can accept and be grateful for every moment I get to experience in my life, or I can choose to obsess about the *why* behind something that happened.

Why didn't it work with that celebrity?! That would have been such a good opportunity! I really, really like him and our connection was strong! Why? Why? Why? Why? Why? Why?

Or I could just say, *I'm so grateful for that experience. Thank you for that, Universe.*

Sometimes I think about what would have happened if things had worked out with me and Cary Grant. If I'd ended up being with him, then I wouldn't be where I am now. And who knows if it would've taken me off my path. Who knows if I would have kept creating videos! Probably not. I don't know. I wouldn't have moved to New York…

I wouldn't have married a Scottish pathological liar…

As the days go by, it's clear that maybe things weren't supposed to work out.

I also had a sober friend tell me, "If you guys were meant to be, you would be. It's that simple. If you were meant to be with him, you would be with him. Things that happen that are meant to be happen with ease and grace. If it's hard, if it's difficult, if it's rigid, that means it's not meant to be." Yes, any relationship will take work down the line, but if a relationship is hard to be in and hurts more than it heals from the beginning, move on!

If you're afraid to move on from a relationship that doesn't serve you, then pray for the courage to do so. Prayer is far more powerful than I ever realized, and I *still* don't use it enough. I pray I start praying more.

16

Meet the Mathewses: Dad

OH, MY PARENTS. They are hilarious, loving, amazing human beings and I love them both dearly! I wouldn't be who I am without their influence, guidance, love, and care. I've waited until this late in the book to talk about them so it'd be easier to see how my upbringing influenced the recent events of my past that I've already covered.

My dad is a hilarious, witty guy. Sometimes he's loud. But he's always goofy. And as of recently, he has no problem telling very sexual jokes that make me cringe. My mom is silly, too—when you listen. She's soft-spoken like me, and when you really pay attention to her, you can hear how funny she truly is. She has this kind of stoner humor that's not super overt, so you might miss it if you're not tapped into the moment.

My parents were all about *The Simpsons* back in the nineties, so I sat and laughed along with them whenever it was on. I feel like most of our family interactions were full of goofiness and comical moments, like we were living in a sitcom. When I think back, it seems like every memory I have with my parents involved our laughing about something. I find that if you have the ability to laugh with the people you're with the most in life, then you're setting yourself up to laugh during even the hard times. That's why I feel so blessed to have such funny parents, and to be funny enough myself to make them laugh a ton still to this day. As I've said, having people around me who make me laugh is one of my top values. And it's because of my parents that this is the case.

When they took me to the beach as a young girl, they would wrap me in a blanket and swing me in it while I screamed and laughed myself to tears. There's an old family video of my dad doing the blanket-swing thing and using it to throw me onto the bed. And I almost hit the window.

"Oh crap!" he yelped. "We're not doing that again!"

They weren't just comical; they were musical Disney-movie parents as well. In the early days, they would sing me off to school: "*We always come back. We'll always come back to get you! Your daddy comes back. He always comes back. He never will forget you!*" In my later years, my mom would wake me up singing "You Are My Sunshine" to me. She has the sweetest voice. Like a little animated movie bunny.

They'd also do this thing where they'd say, "Okay, we're going to wake up the baby dinosaur!" And then I'd pretend to be a baby dinosaur, curling my mouth in weird ways while making animal noises. They'd be all smiles and laugh at my attempt at being ferocious. Clearly, I was their muse.

My dad was the first man I ever loved. He was and is my hero. In my youth, he worked from home a lot even though he had an office on the Disney lot. I think he wanted to be able to spend time with me. He's a screenwriter. He wrote *Peter Pan 2*, *The Little Mermaid 2*, and *Aloha, Scooby-Doo!*, among other fun movies. His being a writer modeled the fact that it was possible to make money being a creative person. It sparked the idea of using my creativity as a career, which might be why I ended up making music videos for girls for money and why I was relentless in my pursuit of comedy and Vine.

Because Dad worked at home, he was always there when I came home from school, which meant I would not get any space as a teenager. All teenagers should go to a far-off land that is safe and AWAY from their parents. Am I right? Needless to say, we butted heads. A lot. I'm a Libra and he's a Taurus, which I think is a deadly combination. He's very stubborn and he always wanted to be right. And then I wanted to be right. Because I equated being right with being loveable, so we would argue often after school. His being irritable and discontent didn't help. Why was he irritable? Maybe it was because he wasn't moving around enough. Maybe sitting around all day writing made him tense. Or maybe he wasn't getting the love he craved from me and my mom. Or maybe it was because, like me, he had a problem with alcohol. Being hungover doesn't exactly lead to Zen energy. He was cranky AF.

My father and I had so many beautiful moments when he wasn't downing his nightly wine. He'd tuck me in at bedtime and tell me stories about this penny that I could take to school with me, and it would always have my back and go on adventures. He called them Penny Stories. One time I woke up to a penny and a note that said: "Take me with you." Other times he would take this stuffed rabbit named Lily and hide behind the wall and use her to talk to me, like something out of *Sesame Street*.

Oftentimes when he slipped out of being the loveable protector who'd tuck me in at night and tell me stories, he would take out his frustrations on me since I was the only one around when Mom was working. I hated arguing with him. I think parents get frustrated at themselves when they don't feel like they're doing a good job, and they can direct that frustration at their children. Unfortunately, I took that to mean that I wasn't loveable enough. One time he threw a book at me. He really valued reading and wanted me to get the same joy that he got out of it. But all I got was hit in the face with a book. JK, it hit the floor. He's not physically abusive or anything, he just REALLY wanted me to read. LOL.

Later in my life, when I was seventeen or eighteen, I was standing in the kitchen and observing him sitting at the table. He started his usual rant and I thought to myself, *Maybe if I don't say anything, things won't escalate...* Because often I would talk back to him. When I did, we'd butt heads. So, this time, I didn't say anything, and he still went from like zero to ten within minutes. It was then that I realized, *Oh... his frustrations have nothing to do with me... He's in pain. He's angry because he's in pain. It's not because of me.*

That was a really powerful realization. I think that as kids, we can take on our parents' negative energy and internalize it, telling ourselves, *I'm not enough. If I were better, they would be happy.* And that is just such a lie!

There was this thing I went to called Insight Seminars at the University of Santa Monica school of spiritual psychology. It was a weekend workshop where we had to explore our minds for clarity on past events. I remember sitting across from this girl and we had to meditate and dive back into our childhood. I had a memory come up of my dad changing my diaper, and I remembered that he got frustrated with himself because maybe he wasn't doing it right. I interpreted that to mean, *I'm frustrating and I'm a burden.* I can't even believe I remembered that, but it goes to show that we can take that energy on without knowing it, even from a time before we have words for what's happening around us.

Growing up thinking that *we* are the problem hinders our growth and our capacity to learn. It causes fear. If parents could become aware of their energies and the messages they are sending to their children and apologize for outbursts brought on by factors such as stress and financial issues, it could go a long way. During those times, my father never apologized for what he did. He would just come into my room and open his arms and expect me to hug him. And I would— resentfully, sometimes.

He never actually said, *"Hey, what I did was wrong and it had absolutely nothing to do with you. Sometimes adults get mad at other things and snap at those around them without thinking about it. I'm sorry. It won't happen again."*

Had he done that, it may have happened a lot less. Because he would have acknowledged his behavior and amended it. He would have been aware that his bad moods had an effect on me. But he didn't, so it kept happening. I'm guilty of that too. No one really taught me to apologize, so I would carry these feelings of guilt for many of my wrongdoings. I would just carry them around and my self-esteem would unknowingly diminish, because I never amended my behavior and said, "*I was wrong when I did that, and here's what I'm going to do to fix things.*"

I think so many of us are suffering from low self-esteem because of things that we've done that we're not cleaning up. We end up carrying all of this weight into our relationships and our jobs because we choose to sweep it all under the rug. But guess what? Our guilt and pain are always there until we amend what caused them. That's why in the twelve-step program there's step eight, where you make a list of all of those people you have harmed, and you choose to become willing to apologize and right whatever wrong you've done to them. Then in step nine you make amends for your behavior.

People's energy completely shifts when you apologize and make up for the ways you've hurt them. I can only speak for myself, but when I went through step nine, the energy around the interaction between me and the person I was apologizing to got so much lighter and better, and I immediately felt a boost in self-esteem.

Not apologizing for harm that I have caused others, no matter how small the transgression, may have been one of the reasons I drank. It's also part of why I ate a lot. I didn't want to deal with my feelings regarding what I had done, so I made myself feel better in other ways. My channel—the term I use for the part of my physical body that my words, ideas, and energy come from—was so filled with alcohol, sugar, and, worst of all, FEAR that I couldn't even see what I was upset about. I had to clear that channel so that I could make room for growth and self-acceptance.

It wasn't until I was writing during step eight that I realized, *Oh... I harmed that person, that person, that person. Oh... I mainly harmed myself. And I owe myself a huge apology.*

That's why I think writing apology letters is really helpful in getting everything out. When we write, the energy from our body comes through our arms onto paper, and we can actually *see* just what has happened—we see all of it at once instead of bit by bit for seconds at a time as it appears in our mind's eye. Seeing your negative actions laid out before you causes a shift in you. It's a very healing thing.

If you're scared to make amends with someone, it might be helpful to know that people are actually more forgiving than you think. I mean, if I could forgive Raymond for what he did, it's likely that people are willing to forgive you for less. Like I said, forgiving him made me feel extremely powerful because it helped heal the energy within me. I was the one holding on to it. So, I could either continue to hold on to it and keep it in my way, blocking myself from moving forward for twenty years, or I could let it go and continue on in my life, enjoying myself. The choice was mine.

The choice is yours, too.

We have to live with ourselves for the rest of our lives. Might as well make best friends and fall in love with ourselves. We're born into this world alone and we we're gonna die alone, but we've got ourselves, so that relationship is the number one relationship. So often we're looking outside ourselves for the love, strength, and validation we already have within us. When it comes from outside of us, it's just a bonus gift.

Since then, my father has apologized to me for his part in our conflicts, as have I to him. I love him very much, and there is nothing I wouldn't do for that man. I am who I am today because of him. He took a stand for me. He was willing to fight against my limited views, because sometimes parents do know more. (And sometimes the kids do.)

What I do know is that my dad did the best he could at the time. He is still a growing human who is learning every day about himself, just like the rest of us. He is not God, and neither am I. We are all doing the best we can. I say all of this to convey that, if you are blessed enough to have a dad, you should go give him a hug or a phone call and tell him you love him. We are quick to blame others for the bad in our lives, but what if we blamed them for the good as well?

So, thank you, Dad, for standing up for me when no one else would. Thank you for teaching me that it's safe to make jokes. Thank you for protecting me and teaching me ways to be creative. Thank you for going to my soccer games and watching me cheerlead for that year when I did that. Thank you, Dad, for smiling and showing up in my life. Thank you for liking and commenting on all of my videos. Thank you for loving me so much and crying in my arms during our father-daughter dance at my wedding. Thank you for holding me when my heart got broken a month later. Thank you for financially supporting me throughout my school years and even some after. Thank you for advising me about what you know and trying to about what you don't. You are a spectacular father. I love you always.

(Cue tears.)

17

Meet the Mathewses: Mom (and Dad Again)

THERE WERE TIMES where I think I may have been close to needing insulin shots, because my mother has always been so gosh-darn sweet. She's like a soft, adorable hamster. That's a compliment, I promise. She's also beautiful. Stunning. Could've been a model if she wanted to be. And I think she really wanted to be. She actually started taking photos at age forty, but I don't think she had the courage—or maybe "confidence" is a better word—to put herself out there in that way. She is really self-conscious about the way she looks even though she is the most beautiful woman I've ever seen.

Fun fact: My mother has another daughter, named Michelle, from a previous marriage, so while I grew up as an only child, I technically have a sister. Mom got married at nineteen and had a daughter at twenty-one. My half-sister, who's twelve years older than me, lives in Kansas City and she has three sons.

Michelle and I are somewhat close. There was one year where we lived together, when she was twenty-three. To tease her, I would always sing the chorus from that Blink-182 song "What's My Age Again?" because it talked about how people don't like you when you're twenty-three. You know, because the nineties...

I remember riding around with her when I was twelve thinking that she was just the coolest girl of all time. We'd listen to Coldplay's song "Yellow." She's actually the one who introduced me to *Friends*, which basically changed my life forever because it made such a big impression on me by delivering my sense of humor almost to a T. I would yell at the dinner table, "Baby Michelle!" sitting right across from her. It always made her laugh. It still does.

Mom was a working woman, so I think I saw that growing up and took it in, using her as an example of something to aspire to—a woman who works for something of her own and contributes to her family. Mom worked at Sony Pictures and then worked at the WB, where she interviewed people like Adam Sandler for *Big Daddy*, Matthew McConaughey for *The Wedding Planner*, Heath Ledger for *A Knight's Tale*, James Franco for *Whatever It Takes*, and Harrison Ford for *Random Hearts*, along with all of the women from the 2000 remake of *Charlie's Angels*. It was around that era. She would interview all of these stars, then the interview would go up on the movie's website. This was around the time the internet first started, so you had to hop on dial-up to see it.

Her job always seemed so cool to me. When I was younger, I thought that it took a lot of courage for someone to interview celebrities. She didn't think so. She always felt comfortable talking to the stars because she always had the mentality that she was equal to them, something I didn't learn until my mid-twenties.

Unbeknownst to my mom, I think she might have played a part in influencing me at the unconscious level like my dad did. I remember being upset and getting fussy on car rides or throughout the day and my mom constantly saying, "Oh, Manon's just hungry." That might be how I developed my overeating issue. From a neurological standpoint, I wired food to feelings. So any time I had a negative feeling, I would just eat, rather than actually checking in by thinking, *Am I hungry or am I upset about something? Did something hurt my feelings?*

If there's one thing I can impart to any new parents who may be reading this, it's that I think it's really important that, when children get fussy, we get in the habit of asking our children, "What is it you want? Are you okay? Are you hungry? Give me a yes or no."

From ages one to seven, children are blank slates from the conscious level to the unconscious. We need to get really specific with them because we're programming them for the rest of their lives in ways they won't even be aware of until the day they end up in front of a therapist. I think it was lucky that I got certified as an NLP (neurolinguistic practitioner) when I was twenty-four and opted to get my master certification two years later. Had I not done that, I'd probably still be an overeater and an overdrinker.

The purpose of the unconscious mind is to protect and control. Those are the only two things the unconscious mind is seeking. Protection and control. If overeating gave me the sensation of protection, comfort, and control because it made me feel better, I need something else to do that for me. I solved my all-or-nothing mentality with one ten-minute hypnosis exercise. Now I don't overeat. And even the thought of having more than one glass of wine makes me sick, because in NLP we delve into the unconscious mind and my NLP teacher gave me other things to do instead to feel full and complete and to make my unconscious stronger. Like, if you take a pacifier away from a kid, you have to replace it with something else. Otherwise the kid will freak out because you took away their source of comfort.

That's why twelve-step programs are such a good solution for a person who drinks, because they're finding comfort through connection in those rooms rather than in a bottle. That connection and validation from something that's not alcohol is what makes those programs so effective and powerful—if you work them. You don't want to go to the gym and just sit there. You have to participate and actually do the work. Daily, too. It's not just a one-and-done thing. If you want clean teeth, you have to brush your teeth every day, twice a day.

I know people who have thirty to forty years' sobriety and they still go to meetings every single day because they are training their "willpower muscles" to stay sober. Because we're such impressionable human beings, even as adults. If I want to drink again, I should probably hang out at a bar. If I want to stay sober, I should frequent meetings. You know?

But I digress…

My parents and I always had a lot of fun together. I'm talking tons of wacky moments and fun family trips. We'd visit Santa Barbara; Seattle, where my dad is from; and Kansas City, where Mom's from. A couple times we went to Hawaii.

All families have a bit of drama. Ours mainly came from me and my dad. But my parents' marriage wasn't without its fair share.

I was eighteen when my mom left my father. It was right after high school, pretty much right when I had just started community college. I never thought they would ever split, even though they both had their issues. They made a great couple! And they were really good for each other in a lot of ways. Hell, even visually they just looked great together.

The night that she left him, we were sitting around watching *American Idol* like we always did. My dad had this thing where he liked to mute or fast-forward the commercials. I think he got irritated—a little too irritated—at one of the commercials because he didn't get to fast-forward or mute it in time or something. And my mom took it for the very last time.

My mom was scared to speak up and use her voice at times. It wasn't that she was scared of him, she just wasn't in her power. She let him dominate her at times, so she felt like she couldn't always speak up. Like, when she and I went shopping and she bought something she liked, she'd tell me, "Don't tell your dad."

So, I had to keep secrets from him. She made him seem scarier than he actually was. Because she would get scared about something that worried her, then I'd see her fear and think, *Oh, he's scary…* Now that I look back, he was just passionate, not scary. It wasn't a big deal at all; it was just something I blew up in my head in my youth, as we often do. This is NOT to invalidate her feelings. A person's energy can feel very heavy to some of us. Both my mom and I are highly intuitive empaths and have to protect ourselves. And at the time, she didn't know that and couldn't get the space she needed to recharge.

So, that night, she got up in a huff and stormed off into the garage. She had a heaviness about her, so I followed her.

She looked at me with hurt and frustration in her eyes and said, "I think I'm going to leave your father."

I nodded and said, "I don't blame you, Mama."

And then she left…

And they divorced.

Right before that, my dad had heart surgery. Right after that, my mom was diagnosed with breast cancer. They're okay and they're both healthy now. In the case of my dad, I think there were some things going unsaid that put a strain on his heart. And the drinking probably didn't help. I think my mom had a hard time loving the parts of Dad that he didn't love. And I think my mom's lack of communication manifested in a way where her body couldn't take care of itself. And my dad's anger manifested in his heart.

My mom got a place near her work. As I mentioned much earlier in this book, I lived with her when I first started at Second City—you know, around the time I got pulled over driving my mom's car, which didn't have automatic lights like mine. And living with my mom? Let me tell you, that aged me. Because we'd watch *The Bachelor* and the show that she called "Big Fat Loser," which was awful because that was definitely not what it was called. You know, because it was actually titled *The Biggest Loser* (which I loved, by the way).

My dad began going to therapy. He started drinking less because I think he was forced to change, which he did. His temperament leveled out quite a bit after the divorce, actually. I remember getting a speeding ticket going to Santa Barbara. I got clocked going eighty-two miles per hour. And I was so terrified to tell him because he used to not take things well. His reactions would be explosive sometimes. And to avoid his going off, lying had become a default response for me, because it wasn't a safe place for me to be honest. This time, however, I was straightforward about it. So, I showed him the ticket, then put my hands in the air in preparation for him to get angry at me. And, to my surprise, he just reacted really calmly for the first time ever. I probably looked like a deer in headlights, like, *Whaaaaaat?* I was so confused, scratching my head. Then I realized what had happened. *Something has shifted in him… He's calmed down a bit.*

Dad and I have spent the last ten years reconnecting. I thought there would always be times when I loathed him for the rest of my days. I thought that we were never going to fully get along. That couldn't have been farther from the truth. I now respect, love, and appreciate what he did for me so much more than I ever did. Had I not had a father who forced me and encouraged me to take theater and choir and to do things that make me feel uncomfortable, I wouldn't be where I am today. I owe him so much that I don't know if I'll ever be able to repay him.

The best part about my wedding day was walking down the aisle with my dad. It was an unreal experience that I'd always wanted to have. And dancing with him during the father-daughter dance was so meaningful that I bawled my eyes out the entire time.

I remember as we started dancing to the song I'd picked, "You Belong to Me" by Carla Bruni, he whispered in my ear, "What song is this?"

"Just listen," I whispered back.

And when he heard it, he felt it to his core and started crying along with me. That was my second-favorite moment of the wedding. If those two moments are all that I got from meeting Raymond, it was all totally worth it.

Despite my parents splitting up, we're all still very close to this day. Sometimes we'll celebrate Thanksgiving, a birthday, or Christmas together. When they're together, it feels like they're a couple. I am beyond grateful that we can all still be in the same room without any animosity.

Their divorce was hard on me. It still kind of is. My dad sold the house, so I don't really have a home base. I had to settle that home base within myself. I had to be like, *Okay, wherever I go, there's my home.* And that's actually made me feel a lot stronger, because now, wherever I go in the world, I always feel safe; home is wherever I am. That definitely helped when I moved to New York. Still, I do kind of wish I had a home to go to, like, a physical home where my parents are there to provide support for me. I kind of feel like it flipped at some point and I somehow became the parent to them. Especially when it comes to my mom. She hasn't had a stable job in years, so Dad and I have been helping support her. I think her leaving my dad without confronting him is what got her there in the first place; it took a toll on her self-esteem. I think she hasn't felt good enough in the last ten years to put herself out there and get a job. Sometimes when people get older, they let their age limit their ideas about what they can do. I know my mother can do anything, but SHE has to be the one to believe. Age will only hold you back if you let it.

The best part about everything that has come out of my Vine days is the fact that I am fortunate enough to be able to afford to take care of my parents the way they did for me. My mom's car was really old and I overheard her one day talking about how she liked red cars. So, when I could afford it, I bought her a red 2017 Chevy Cruze and filmed her reaction to the surprise sitting outside of her house. She was over the moon, and it really warmed my heart that I was able to do that for her.

I took Mom on an unforgettable trip to Ireland, where I drove us on the opposite side of the road and surprisingly didn't get us into any accidents! The roads were incredibly narrow, so it wasn't the easiest to get around. But it was very much worth the adventure. We stayed in different bed-and-breakfasts. One B & B belonged to this guy named Thomas Walsh. He said he was sober, but every night the scent of weed would start wafting into our room. He would smoke downstairs and it would seep through the vents. The definition of "sober" is different for everyone, I suppose. In the mornings he would cook us eggs and talk about how his friend turned into a reptile in front of his eyes. He said she finally showed him her true self and that her skin turned to bluish-green scales. And we'd just be sitting there at the kitchen table responding, "Great... More coffee, please?"

When we hit Cork, Ireland, we kissed the Blarney Stone. We ran around making Vines. My mother is such a good sport. We went to the Cliffs of Moher, which are the most beautiful sight I've ever seen. It was really special to get to do that with my mother. I feel really, really grateful that Vine and the brand deals that followed afforded me the ability to give us an experience like that.

Thank you, Mother, for all of your love and kindness. Thank you for being so beautiful to look at. Thank you for teaching me that it is better to be kind than to be right. Thank you for teaching me how to listen and hold space for people. Thank you for making me laugh and always playing along with me. Thank you for always supporting me emotionally. Thank you for passing down your awesome fashion sense (you can still be a model, if you want to). Thank you for being the easiest person to be around. Thank you for reminding me that it's what's inside that matters. Thank you for being my friend. You've been a dream of a mother, and I feel like I hit the jackpot with you.

My parents are both supportive people who have a lot of love to give, and I like to think that they're both very proud of me and the woman I became. And I hope I can keep making them proud.

This chapter and the previous one are for you, Mom and Dad. Thank you so much for all your love and support over the years.

18

The Centaur

THERE WERE A few times in my life where I had interesting moments with older men. Not bad; interesting. There's one experience that's definitely worth sharing, because it was definitely worth having, as strange as it was.

It was a few years before I moved to New York. This very tall older guy was always hanging around this one tree on my street. It's less creepy than it sounds; I get why he would spend time there. It was in a beautiful spot with gorgeous-looking trees that made you feel like you were in a magical fairyland! Oh, how I wish that existed.

I also used to see him a lot on one of the hiking trails near my house. When I was hiking alone or with a friend, he'd often come trotting up; between his height and his energy, he reminded me of a centaur, one of those half-horse, half-man mythological creatures. I don't know how he always seemed to find me. The more I think about it, the more I'm wondering if he was a stalker. Let's say for the sake of this story that he was a normal dude who wasn't following me. Okay, cool...

One day I saw him rolling toward me on his bicycle. He climbed off and began walking up to me (cue slow-motion special effect), pulling his bike alongside him. This guy walked up real close and started listening in on the conversation my friends and I were having. At that point I knew a little about him from my neighbors, like that he was a Green Beret. It's not like I knew him well, but I knew enough for it to feel somewhat normal for him to be standing there. While the group of us were chatting, he leaned right up to my ear and said, "I'm very attracted to you." Then he just backed away. I stared at him in silence, unsure of what I was supposed to say. I wasn't used to that from anyone.

Buy me a drink first, sir! Ask me out to coffee or something. That's very forward… or is it? I don't freakin' know!

After waiting for a moment, he finally went on to say, "I know I'm a lot older than you, but I just wanted you to know how beautiful you are."

Sure, that caught me off guard, but I didn't let his uncanny advance stop me from saying yes when he *did* ask me out.

Our first date was dinner and a movie. After we left the theater, we decided to have a seat at a table outside the Starbucks that was on the way to the parking lot. He asked me a few questions and then began looking at me with longing in his eyes. He paused, then told me: "You're a bird… You're a free bird."

I just smiled in confusion, like, *Umm, what?*

I knew that was true. I feel like I am a bird, so I did feel like he saw me. But at the same time, my logical mind was thinking, *Dude, you don't know me!*

After the bird comment, we continued on to my car. I got behind the wheel, and he climbed into the passenger seat. Without hesitation and with total conviction, he told me he loved me.

Holy shit. I barely know this guy, and yet my whole body is tingling from the intensity of his emotions and candidness! WTF is happening here?! The parking lot outside of the movie theater after our first date together is not a great time to declare that, buddy…

I heard him, let him feel that. I felt something too—not love, but some sort of vibration all over my body. *Maybe he's a reptile! Who knows!*

And, after all of that, we got intimate. Ya know… he told me he loved me and everything! HA.

After we fooled around, he *saged* me. Like, he lit a bundle of sage and passed it all over my body.

Huh… ? I just sat there, stunned, confused. *Where did he even get the sage from? He came out and it was already lit! Was he planning the sageing? Aren't you supposed to sage someone before intertwining, not after? Is he purifying me from himself?*

I accidentally left a bracelet there, and he probably, like, kept it to use for some sort of ritual. I don't know what he might have done with it, but I know that I never wanted to get it back from him because that experience was *very* overwhelming.

The really weird part of his dropping the whole "You're a bird" line is that something really odd and coincidentally related happened later that week.

I was cruising along Topanga Canyon from the beach with my friend Amy, with the windows open and the music blasting. We heard a loud boom, then a split second later something whacked me on the head.

"Ouch! What was that?" I yelped, pulling over. Then I looked around, nervously searching for whatever I'd just hit. "What the hell was that? You heard that, right?"

"Yeah, I heard that!" Amy shouted. "I don't know!"

"It felt like whatever it was hit me in the head!" And that's when I looked down and found a dead bird on the center console… A freaking SPARROW hit the car, then hit me in the head and died in my car.

That's so weird… That centaur said I was a bird, I thought as I mildly freaked out over that poor little bird.

Little signs like that are very important to look out for. I'm not sure what it meant, but that coincidence was too coincidental to not be a sign about something.

The centaur soldier would call me often after we went out together. Of course, I didn't always pick up. One time he left me four four-minute messages. I should have ended it right then and there, because that is TOO MUCH. Other times he would send me voice memos that were, like, thirty minutes long, where he'd tell me things like, "You're one in a million… You need to put yourself out there…" and all of these other things. "Intense" would be the best way to describe him and the way he went about things.

There was one time where we were on a hike and he grabbed my hand, then tugged me along to the top of the hill and started making out with me. I went along with all of it, feeling like I just didn't have a choice in the matter (not in a bad way), until I suddenly broke free, thinking to myself, *This is crazy! Who even is this person?*

Thinking back on it all, he may have had some mental issues… But it's an experience that I can't regret, because it gave me a fun story to tell my little ones someday. Actually, I probably shouldn't.

Then again, whatever… they can read it in here.

It can take a lot of the pressure away when we realize that life can be looked at as a series of experiences. They mean what we make them mean. When I do things that I'm afraid of, I just look at it like, *This is just an exercise, this is just practice for future experiences.* That lightens the load a bunch for me. But remember what I said about signs. If you want to change your life, then notice the experiences that stand out and give them attention; they may be able to guide you as you grow and transform.

At the end of the day, all we have is our memories and our experiences. When I'm old, I'm probably not going to regret the things that I did. I'm going to regret the things that I *didn't* do. So, I try to do everything I can and try to experience as much as possible—provided I'm not putting myself in certain danger (which I've clearly done anyway… but I'm stopping now!).That's why I bungee-jump from bridges and have sex with people who sage me. Feel out the energy of each situation that arises, and if there are no negative vibes, ask yourself, *If not now, when?*

When I was younger, I used to really worry about certain labels or being judged and all these really insignificant things. Eventually I realized, *I'm so worried about who I'm sleeping with right now, but I have like eighty years left if I'm lucky, so why can't I just live my life and enjoy every connection while I can?*

Let's just judge ourselves less and enjoy the moment and not make it mean anything negative. Maybe we can enhance each experience as much as possible and celebrate life. Maybe we can decide to take everything as a gift rather than view some experiences as a reason for regret.

I just feel like people are too hard on themselves and too hard on others, and it doesn't make space for us to grow and experience life to the fullest. Everyone is so scared and rigid and stressed, even when they still have youth and vigor. The next thing we know, we may end up being sickly before we even get a chance to grow old and die. We need to enjoy every moment we have. We need more love and tolerance and passion.

After someone says, *"Hey, I did this crazy thing..."* rather than saying, *"What? You did what?"* let's try to get in the habit of saying, *"Oh wow! And how was it? How did that experience make you feel?"* Let's criticize less and focus more on what we are taking from the experiences we have.

Remaining curious is so beneficial for the unconscious mind. It generates more questions and allows more learning experiences to take place. Being judgmental of ourselves and others hinders something in us and the people around us. It cuts us off from new experiences by making us fear the idea of taking risks and trying new things.

When I'm conversing with someone and they're telling me a story, I often like to ask, "What else? And what else?" rather than "Why?" Why doesn't really matter. You can spend twenty years asking why about something and never find the answer. Like me with that Sparrow (not the Johnny Depp kind). Why did that bird hit me in the head and die in my car after that centaur of a man said that I was a bird? That's something I may never know. And even if or when we do find out the answers to the many whys of life, it probably won't do us any good. But the questions "What else?" and "What did you learn from that?" and "What will you do differently next time?" are important because they add to our quality of life rather than take away from it. "How?" is a really productive question, too. "How did I get here?" "How can I learn from this?" and "How can I change now that this happened?" are all more productive questions than why.

Remember, dear reader: "You're a bird... you're a free bird" too. Enjoy your life and take in as many positive experiences as you can. Use each one as a stepping stone toward growth, or at the very least, get a good story out of taking chances.

But don't let anyone do any postcoital sageing on you.

Or do... Whatever you're into. It's your life, after all!

19

@MeIsRussell

RUSSELL CAME AT the perfect time in my life, which is funny because I didn't even want a dog. It's not that I don't like dogs, it's just that I've suffered from dog allergies since I was young. Raymond made sure to always bring up how he wanted a dog and add, "But we'll never have one, because you're allergic…"

At the beginning of 2020, after I finally came to terms with the end of my relationship, this wave of wanting love in my life again came over me. First, I looked up mini pigs. I had an obsession with baby pigs for years. I followed like ten teacup pigs on Instagram, and every time one came up on my feed, I just felt so much love! I love their cute little snouts and the way they sound when they run on wood, and the oinking noises that they make. It fills my heart! So, when this urge for love came over me, I thought, *Hmm, I won't be allergic to a baby pig, so I should get a pig!*

My friend Shannon, who was my roommate at the time, found a place deep in the Valley that was raising pigs to be pets. She and I ventured out there to check it out and found ourselves at this house that was a complete sketchy mess. A pigsty. Literally. All of these pigs came to the gate, and each one of them was large and dirty. Some were smaller but far from teacup.

A young, skinny girl with green hair came up to us with one of the younger pigs. "This one is a new pig that we have," she said.

"Well, I thought these were going to be little *baby* pigs," I said.

"They are baby pigs. These are all six months."

"What about the little, tiny teacup pigs?"

"Oh, there's no such thing as teacup pigs. They're a myth."

"But… I've seen them online…"

Apparently, if you get a baby pig, there's no way of actually knowing how big it's going to get. That was a little disappointing to hear. And after being around that pigsty and seeing how dirty those pigs were, I figured I might as well get myself a little dog instead.

That night after the pigsty, I kept picturing the kind of dog I wanted. When I went on set the next day, I ended up searching "hypoallergenic dogs" and found someone selling Yorkie puppies for $3,000. *Yeah… that's a little too expensive for me. Maybe I should adopt.*

I quickly backed out and added "for adoption" to my "hypoallergenic dog" search query. That's when I found they were having an adoption day at Tailwaggers on Franklin from 11:00 A.M. to 2:00 P.M. the next day!

Oh, that's perfect, I'll go look at dogs. No pressure.

Shannon tagged along with me, and so did my mom. As soon as we walked in, we saw a bunch of dogs running around, playing. As I scanned the room filled with adorableness, I turned around, and in the corner, I saw a blond girl holding this little brown puppy that had two other colors in his coat. He was just the most beautiful puppy I had ever seen, and I was instantly drawn to him. I hurried right over to the little guy, grabbed him (gently), held him, and said, "I want this one!"

That's right, I stole a puppy from a little girl. Just kidding. She was done with him. But if she hadn't been…

This is my dog, I thought as I gave him rubs and played with him. I didn't even have time to think. I just knew. And the people there knew he was mine because other people kept coming up to him and I started getting really protective. When other people would inquire, I wanted to growl at them. There was one lady whose finger I bit off when she tried to touch him. *Ruff!*

I named him Russell. Why? Because someone said that name at some point in our interaction and I thought, *I love the name Russell! And he does kind of look like a Russell.* So, it stuck.

The next thing I knew, I was signing papers, then I was paying the $430 adoption fee. After going shopping around the store for pee pads and toys, all of a sudden, I was taking home a puppy! Not even just a younger dog. A puppy. A three-pound, two-month-old puppy! My mom didn't try to stop me. She didn't warn me what I was in for.

Shannon was like, "Oh, I'll help you take care of the little guy." As I'm writing this chapter in February 2020, I currently live alone because Shannon has just moved out. She did help me for, like, a month, so I guess she technically didn't lie, but still…

That first night, I was so happy I had a pup to love and who would love me. It was one of the best nights of my life. Yet it was also kind of the worst. Because, later that night, I was up when I would normally have been sleeping because I was trying to crate-train Russell. It took just a few hours past bedtime for me to go all doom and gloom.

What the hell did I just do? My whole life is going to be different! I must have been out of my mind when I thought this was a good idea!

The next day, I was shooting a pilot, so I brought Russell to set with me. Everyone fell in love with him. Here I was, not even twenty-four hours into having him, and I was like, "If you love him so much, you can have him! I'm thinking of giving him away." I hate admitting that, but it's the truth.

I was legitimately asking around seeing who wanted a puppy, because it all just hit me. *Wait… What am I going to do with him when I travel? What happens if I end up filming later than expected? I can't leave him alone for too long! What am I doing?*

The people whom I vented my concerns to kept saying, "It's okay! It'll be worth it! Just stick it out!"

My friend Johnny told me, "How about you wait until Tuesday to make your decision. Don't think about it right now."

Okay. I can stick it out a few days.

About a week in, I was madly in love with Russell and I was beating myself up for ever considering giving him away because I couldn't fathom what life would be like without him! I don't think I had ever understood the intense, obsessive bond people have with their pets. It always went over my head. I would see dogs out and think, *Oh, they're cute.* But I wouldn't obsess like some people I saw.

Now that it's been a month, I can totally say that I am one of those obsessed dog moms who stare at pictures and videos of their pup. My now-seven-pound Morkie-huahua (my name for a Maltese-Yorkie-Chihuahua mix) brings me nothing but joy, and I'm so much happier with him in my life! Like, the second I leave the house for errands or filming or whatever, I'm so excited to rush home to see him and cuddle him and kiss him and take photos of him. It's nuts to think that if all goes well, he'll be in my life for the next fifteen years!

Russell sleeps through the night now, which is great. I love waking up to him in the morning. I love all the kisses from my cuddle monster. Sometimes Russell goes a little crazy, jumps at my face, and bites me a ton, but apparently, he'll outgrow that. I guess I'll have to put up with getting my face nipped for a few more weeks. Or months...

It was only after having Russell come into my life that I understood the idea behind service animals and emotional support animals. I always feel like I'm in such a meditative state when I look at him, because he has all of my focus and I'm not in my head. I wonder if maybe we all need a service animal or two to help achieve inner peace, so that we can be better at being of service to others.

I wouldn't trade him for the world. It's funny what fear can say to us. I feel so confident now that this is a stepping stone for me to one day have kids. I really want a full house of them, as I was an only child. My biggest dream is to be a mother. I feel I've been training the last eight years for it. Spending thousands of dollars to grow so I can be the best mother I can be for my future children. My prediction is that I'll have two. A boy and a girl. If that happens, then we will know that ManonFesting works or that I'm psychic.

20

~~The Last Chapter~~
The Next Chapter

*S*O, WHAT'S NEXT *for Manon Mathews?*

Well, I'm working toward becoming a full-time film and TV director. I just finished starring in my second feature film. Every day I'm continuing to build myself up from the fallout of my marriage. I'm always getting ready for something new. But my lifelong goal will be to focus on what's good so I can enjoy my fulfilling life as a human on this earth. To be of service as much as I can by cracking jokes, whether in person or on camera, on the big screen or on TikTok—that will continue to be a daily goal. This book is my way of being of service to you, because I've shared all of these stories not to say "look at me" but to give you a better understanding of who I am and also in hopes that it may help people who are struggling with making their dreams come true, or suffering with addiction, or going through relationship issues, or dealing with past trauma. This book is my attempt at letting you know that it's funny how it works out when you put yourself out there, change for the better, and truly go after what it is you want out of life!

This last chapter is a reminder that if you're going through something difficult right now, it WILL pass. I promise you that. Every day can be an opportunity to start fresh. This is just a short period in your life, and you *will* find hope and good things if you persevere and keep getting back up after stumbling during your journey down the road of life. Which you will... because we all fall at some point. You are NOT alone. And if you need help with that, check out the bonus section, "Lessons in ManonFestation," for some therapeutic tips that I've learned along the way. Some tips are practices I use daily (even when things are good) to keep me on track toward manifesting the life I'm still working for. Others I use to get through rough spells.

For many, many years, I thought that finding the right man would be the only thing that would make me complete. How could I not be whole after finding the love of my life—my soulmate, right? Again, if a soulmate is one's other half, how could finding them not complete you? It wasn't until after having incredibly exciting and sometimes excruciatingly painful experiences and after years of working on myself and after countless hours of studying techniques in self-improvement that I finally learned that, in order to be complete, I must accept and learn to love myself first. I learned that every day is a process of loving the girl in the mirror. Only after we learn to love and accept ourselves will we be able to be ready for a relationship with "the one," once we find them. And that's the message I would like to leave you with.

It's been a ~~hell~~ heaven of a journey. Thank you for being a part of it!

LESSONS

IN

MANONFESTATION

Lesson 1
Get Silly!

A question I often get is, *"Manon, how do you deal with stress?"*

The best way for me to deal with stress and the many external pressures of life is to not take myself so seriously. When I get stressed out, the first thing I do is find something that makes me laugh. I spend time with funny people or I watch something funny. And if I can't find something to make me laugh, I get silly so I can laugh at myself! Laughter is the best medicine; it relieves tension.

Guess what? We only get one life. Not only do we get only *one*, but our time on Earth is short and can be stripped away at any moment. It might also help for you to know that whatever is causing you stress is probably not a personal attack on you.

The best thing anyone has ever said to me when I was complaining about someone else was, "It's not about you! None of this is about you!" Meaning, the way a person behaves has less to do with you and more to do with them.

Thank God!

When I realized that the world doesn't revolve around *me*, things became easier in my life. Everything stopped feeling so weighted. I stopped feeling delicate. If you truly know that most things are not about you, then you're free from the restraints that *you* are putting on yourself.

Stop taking life so seriously. Life can feel hard sometimes, but we don't have to make it more difficult by thinking the world is out to get us. It's not. I promise. Sometimes we worry about what other people think about us, when the truth is, more than likely no one is thinking about you. Everyone is thinking about themselves.

Take nothing personally. Take life easy. Laugh often. Get silly every chance you get, to remind yourself to enjoy this journey we're on.

Lesson 2
Get It Out!

When I see people all happy and I'm not feeling happy, it kind of pisses me off. Like, *Why can't I be as happy as them?!*

It's not their fault that I'm down. Cheery people should be allowed to be walking around all happy! But why does it piss me off? Because there's something in *me* that I haven't dealt with yet. Usually, it's sorrow or anger. And do you know what helps me work through it? Writing it all down on paper! Write all your feelings out. EVERYTHING. Getting that stuck energy out through the arms onto the paper is essential for a shift in perspective to happen. Write it out, even if it takes ten pages. Or ten hours! Well, hopefully it won't take ten hours… Maybe shoot for twenty minutes. Then you can burn what you write like you're having a nice cleansing ceremony with candles and whatnot. Sadness and anger are there for a reason. Acknowledging them and addressing them in a physical form, like writing your feelings down, helps us to heal from what's hurting inside.

It's good to get out our emotions and not bottle anything in. If you don't like to write, find a close friend or relative you can talk to whom you trust so you can get out your true, honest feelings. We are all human beings and everyone has feelings, so go easy on yourself and know that it's okay to express your emotions. You don't need to hold on to them alone!

The sooner we address our feelings and get them out, the sooner they will pass.

Lesson 3
Get Moving!

Get moving. Move, move, move! Somewhere down the line, we forgot that motion affects our emotions. Our bodies are meant to move. Animals are always roaming and playing. Our ancestors were nomads who used to walk like twelve miles per day. We as a species didn't get sedentary until the rise of office jobs. Getting out of the house feels good, and seeing the world beyond our homes and work distracts us from our feelings. Why? Because our bodies are meant to move!

When I moved to New York, I walked so much that I instantly became happier and my quality of life increased significantly. The good news is you can get moving whether you feel like it or not. If you're lying there thinking, *I don't feel like moving, I'm so tired*, forget about your feelings! Don't think about it, just do it. We can think our way out of doing anything, even the things that are good for us. If you need to give yourself a countdown, then do it. Three. Two. One. GO! Put this book down and get up! Go for a walk and resume reading later. You don't have to go outside if it's too late; just pace around your home.

If you change your physical state, you change your mental state. Humans are meant to move, and things like work, studying, and bingeing TV shows make us spend so much time sitting still. Even if it's a walk around your workplace or around the neighborhood, do it as often as you can. Listen to a song that moves you if you need some help getting motivated! Or listen to something that makes you want to dance.

Speaking of which, DANCE! Get up and do it! It's going to be really hard for you to be sad if you're dancing. Have you ever seen a sad dancer? Actually, I have and it's very funny to watch... but that's beside the point. When you're home alone, get up, blast some music, and do a goofy dance. It'll be hard to keep from laughing if you're being silly and watching yourself going hard for no reason.

Lesson 4
Do What Makes You Happy!

Find what makes you happy and DO those things. What a concept, right? It's so silly that we spend eight hours a day or more doing things that we don't want to do—like commuting or working. And, don't get me wrong, hard work is a great thing and doing what you need to do to pay your bills is important. But sometimes we do things because we think we *should* do them rather than because we want to. Because maybe we feel like the things we love, like hobbies, are a waste of time or there's not enough time in the day for leisure. But I'm here to tell you that we *NEED* to find time for the things we love.

Not everything we do in life is going to be something we love doing. But there ought to be at least one thing in the day that we do because we love it. Maybe don't wait two years to start a spirituality channel or wait four years to start that book you've always wanted to write (like I did). Take a few minutes a day. Block off a nice thirty minutes to an hour to do what you want. Because if we're not doing things that we love doing during our time on this earth, then what are we doing? Really.

I get stuck on this all the time. We do things because we think we *should* and we avoid what we are passionate about because we think we *should* make time for crucial things. I hate that word. "Should."

Why don't you stop shoulding all over yourself...?

There is no should. There's just what is. Do what you want to do. Fulfill your purpose. People like to be around positive, happy people. And the people who are positive and happy are like that because they're filling up their lives with joyful things. When I'm not happy, it's because I'm not doing things that make me feel good. You know what I'm saying?

So, stop shoulding around and do something that brings you joy before you start reading the next lesson.

Unless reading is what you truly enjoy. Then, by all means…

Lesson 5
Be Grateful!

Did I thank you for picking up a copy of this book? Because thank you! It makes me so happy that you wanted to read about my journey and that you are (hopefully) taking something positive away from what you've read so far. And speaking of thanks... I'm going to talk a little bit about gratitude.

A quote that I love from Oprah Winfrey goes like this: "What you focus on expands, and when you focus on the goodness in your life, you create more of it. Opportunities, relationships, even money flowed my way when I learned to be grateful no matter what happened in my life." And I live by that.

Focusing on what we have gives us more of what we want. It makes us appreciate the good more. It's the best way to get in a better mood instantly. The other thing is that we *DO* have a choice in what we focus on; we just have to use that power for good and work with instead of against ourselves.

You can't be in entitlement and gratitude at the same time. You can't be in fear and love at the same time. You have to choose! You get to choose! Moment to moment. Sometimes I think maybe we don't know that we can choose, so we go to our default emotion.

So, I choose gratitude today! Because if I focus on what I have, then I'm going to get more of that. If you focus on what you don't want, you will get more of that. If you focus on what you love and what you're grateful for, you will get more of that good stuff.

I'm grateful for my legs, because they let me walk and dance.

I'm grateful for the sunshine in Los Angeles.

I'm grateful for my health (especially in the time of coronavirus).

I'm grateful for my phone, because it provides entertainment and the ability to communicate with those I love and with all of you.

I'm grateful that I have a voice and a platform that I can use to help others laugh and grow.

I am super grateful that I have a heart that beats and that I am alive.

Focus on the good! Always.

Lesson 6
Be Nice to You!

The way we speak to ourselves is of the utmost importance. Being kind to ourselves can make or break our day. Being kind to others starts with us first! The more we practice being kind to ourselves, the more natural it will be to be kind to others. The same is true in reverse.

How do we talk to kids and babies?

Sweet voice "Hi, how are you! Aw, you're so cute!"

What if we talked to ourselves that way? Wouldn't that just be so much better?

"Aw, [insert your name here], aren't you just the most beautiful thing in the world!"

But no, so many of us are programmed and habituated to talk to ourselves in such a mean, cruel way. We have the highest expectations of ourselves, then we end up being highly critical of ourselves, like, *You son of a bitch! How did you mess that up? You can't do anything right!*

One helpful tip that I learned from neurolinguistic programming is to listen to what you say to yourself. When you catch yourself saying something mean, change the voice! For instance, if you're telling yourself, *I can't do this… I don't feel good about myself,* replay that negative thought out loud, but in a Mickey Mouse voice. Try saying something you're insecure about out loud right now in your best Mickey Mouse impression. Sounds pretty ridiculous, right? Well, that's how ridiculous the voices in our heads sound. And if we say it in a silly voice, we don't respond to it the same way.

We needn't take our thoughts so seriously. Don't believe everything you think! Unless it's a good, wonderful, beautiful thought about yourself. That, you can believe. How we speak to ourselves is so important. Treat yourselves with kindness so you can heal and, in doing so, you can treat others with kindness.

Remember, kind people don't harm people. Only hurt people hurt people.

Lesson 7
I'ma Do It Anyway!

We're always going to have thoughts. We can't get away from them, nor do we need to. We can simply observe them and thank them for stopping by. What you resist persists, so don't resist them. Rather, allow them to come and pass through. Maybe even be kind to them!

Sometimes we think of things and then become attached to that thinking. Like, *Okay, here's this sort of negative thing that popped into my head and I'm going to fixate on it and let it stop me from doing what I want.*

No! Don't fixate on every thought, but also don't ignore them. Try just evaluating each one, like, *Oh, that's an interesting thought. Why do I feel that way?*

Eckhart Tolle talks a lot about that kind of nonattachment. We don't have to attach to every thought. We don't have to follow each one down the rabbit hole. Like, if it's time to exercise, most of the time I don't want to. So, if I hear a voice in my head say, *I don't want to work out*, I respond, *Thank you for sharing... I'm just going to put on my shoes and do it anyway.*

The whole *I'm going to do it anyway* mentality has literally been the way I've done anything, especially things I don't like or that are outside of my comfort zone. That's how I got through improv. That's how I get up onstage when I'm having doubts. We don't need to resist the voices or the thoughts. Just allow them in and only follow through on the ones that lead to self-betterment and good experiences.

Lesson 8
Rest!

Resting is *OKAY*! It's actually great! Go to bed early. Take a nap. Take breaks as much as possible.

I don't let myself rest as much as I probably could. So, today I'm practicing giving my body that break that it needs to restore itself to optimal health. Just like a cell phone needs to be charged, we need sleep and rest to restore our energy. In order for me to be my best, I need to rest. Even a quick meditation does the trick.

When you're tired, learn to rest, not to quit! At times, I get very tired from all the traveling, performing, creating, and filming I do, so I take breaks to rejuvenate myself. The last pose in yoga after all the hard work is the one where you lie down and let everything sink in nicely. If we go, go, go, we're going to wear ourselves out and then tire out or get sick. And I ain't about to get sick! The body is so smart it will sometimes create illness just to force us to slow down.

Oftentimes, we'll judge ourselves for resting, like, *Oh, I'm being lazy! There's no time to rest! I'll rest when I'm dead!*

But rest is essential for your body, mind, and spirit. Life is always moving at such a fast pace nowadays. I can't keep up! I don't want to keep up! And you don't have to either! The judgment that we're not doing enough inflicts pain on us that we don't need. We need not judge. We need just love. And resting is showing love to yourself. Stop neglecting yourself and telling yourself that you're too busy. Make time to show yourself some love in the form of a break or sleep. Listen to your body. Ask yourself, *Do I need to rest?* If the answer is yes, then do it! You deserve it! You may now give yourself that permission.

Lesson 9
Every Day Is a Holiday!

"Every day is a holiday and every meal is a banquet."

I heard a man say that once and I loved it! It reminds us that our experience of the world is a state of mind. How come over the holidays we're allowed to feel amazing and good and eat whatever we want? How come when Monday rolls around and it's time to go back to real life, the happiness fades?

Monday... Bleh... People just cringe at that word. Then when it's Friday we let ourselves celebrate.

Monday is just a word. It's just a state of mind. But if we're not aware of it, how would we know? But now we know!

On a recent Monday, I thought to treat it like a Friday. I went to Starbucks and this girl was upset and complaining that it was Monday. I told her, "What if we pretend that it's Friday?!"

She did, and we started dancing together, her behind the counter and me in line. Because we're allowed to dance on a Monday! Or anytime! Remember, *we* actually get to choose how we feel. So even when I'm not feeling well or having a bad day, I can still go write a gratitude list and be grateful to be alive. I can choose to be happy in any moment.

What a concept, right? It takes practice. It's not just going to happen after you finish reading this in one go. I mean, it might for you. Even if you don't feel it, you can just say it.

"Today I feel happy!"

Say that, and it will change the way you feel. Or you can smile for sixty seconds. And then it'll turn into a natural smile.

Joy is often a state of mind. Following my feelings as a kid wasn't a good idea at times, because I was often sensitive and I would tell myself that I wasn't happy. The thing about that is, the mind is always listening and will create events to prove you right. So even if it feels unnatural in the beginning to say to yourself, "Today I feel great!" or "Today is a holiday," keep repeating it and you will reprogram your mind to change its perspective. Repetition is the key to learning, after all.

Lesson 10
Express Yourself!

The inception of this lesson came to me while I was doing some self-care and putting on a face mask. Sometimes it's just good to do a nice deep cleanse with a face mask, or a deep diet cleanse. It's also good to do an emotional cleanse, so don't bottle your feelings up. Dance it out! Sing it out! Cry! Get it all out of your body and your mind. If we don't express our authentic selves, then it's likely that our bottled-up emotions will get trapped in the body, possibly resulting in illness.

When I was younger, I was told that I was "too sensitive." Because of that I decided it was a good idea to push all my feelings down and keep them there.

"Don't cry, Manon!"

"Don't burden others with your pain."

Blah blah blah.

If you need to cry, cry. It's okay. It's beautiful. It's human. It's okay to be open about being sad. It's just an energy release. Energy has to flow, or the pressure will build and build until it explodes in some negative way. That's how migraines and stomach ulcers happen. (This is like the fifty-seventh time I've talked about illness, but I'm repeating it for a reason!)

As the brilliant Eckhart Tolle writes, "Whatever you think the world is withholding from you, you are withholding from the world." So don't be a goof and hold back what's inside you. The songs you want to sing, the dances you want to do in the middle of the street, the ideas for inventions, that book you always wanted to write, the truth you want to speak, the emotions you want to release—share them with the world. Let them out!

Everything matters. Full self-expression is crucial to happiness and growth. Express yourself to people and to yourself. Get clear on what you're feeling and what's going on within your mind, because it may not always be clear what's wrong until you talk it out or write about it. If you're feeling a certain way about someone and you can't communicate with them, remember, they're not a mind reader. Just because you're laying down hints and putting out signs, that doesn't mean the person you're trying to tell something to is going to get the message. Let's be clear with the people in our life; we—and they—deserve that.

The pain that we feel is usually about what we don't say. It's hardly ever really about another person. Everybody is doing the best that they can to take care of themselves, so it's your job to do the same!

Don't judge your feelings; just be honest with yourself about them. It's worth it. And if you're feeling anger, I encourage you to go deeper to see what's really going on, because anger usually covers fear and sorrow. Just a thought!

Lesson 11
Take off That Mask!

Whether we're aware of it or not, I think many of us are wearing "masks" at times when we're not alone. It could be pounds of makeup, a wig, changing our hair color, acting differently around different groups of people, or showing off with fashion—we're just covering our true natures and the true beauty that the universe gifted us with. We're just hiding who we truly are!

Have you ever noticed someone who's trying too hard or a fake, and suddenly you feel a pit in your stomach like something is off? The probable reason for this is that they're not being authentic. That's why we love babies and animals so much. It's because they can't help being who they are. As we age, we become self-aware and adopt other people's beliefs and fears. We start losing trust that who we really are is enough. And I'm telling you right now that *you, dear reader, are enough*! I am enough. We're all enough just as we are, because we're walking around this planet, and being here is all that we need to be loveable.

So, if you've been wearing a mask, try going the day without it. Unveil yourself and trust in all of the things about you that make you amazing, and see what happens! It might be uncomfortable, but you'll see that that icky feeling will pass.

Just try it. Let the world see you and love you.

(Except during a pandemic. Wear that mask!)

Lesson 12
Breathe! Or Cry!

I have breakdowns sometimes… in public. There was one brisk January morning when I was living in Manhattan and I had a breakdown on the subway train. I imagine that's not uncommon in New York, because no one really reacted to my sobbing on a fairly crowded subway car.

Getting overstressed happens sometimes. We're all human and, therefore, all prone to it. So rather than acting as if life never overwhelms us, why don't we express ourselves accordingly? Sometimes a good cry is all we need. Maybe you don't feel comfortable having a breakdown in a public area. That's okay! Find a bathroom, or wait until you get home and you feel safe expressing your feelings. If you're unable to get home quickly enough, just find yourself a quiet place where you can take a few deep breaths.

Breath work is surprisingly calming as well. What I like to do is breathe in for five counts, hold for five, then exhale for five. I repeat that five times, and it relaxes me.

Saying prayers also helps. Getting in touch with my higher power usually brings me back to a moment of love. Love is healing. Sometimes I even like to shake my booty. Whatever it takes to change my state immediately, I do it! Someone once told me, "Tears are just ice melting from your heart." A little cheesy, but true. Crying is okay! It's just energy releasing. Just like laughing.

Remember, there ain't no shame in cryin'!

Lesson 13
Don't Settle!

Relationships. It's my favorite subject. Life is really just a series of experiences and a web of relationships. I'm asked a lot about how to deal with breakups. If you read this book, you know some of my thoughts on that already, but I'll touch on it again.

First of all, if you're looking for *the one*, the *right one*, then you got to get out of the *wrong one*. If you're in a toxic relationship, if you don't feel quite right about who you are with, if you think there's something more out there for you—don't settle. I spent three magical, wonderful years with myself. That helped me learn and grow and be okay when things didn't work out with a relationship, because I didn't need anybody. Being single and falling in love with ME is how I started to really learn what I wanted and what I didn't want in a partner. I suggest making a list of every single thing that you want so that your mind is clear on what to look for. That time alone gave me the clarity to distinguish if something new was right or wrong, good for me or not good for me.

We want to be loved, and that's okay. And if you want to have fun, have fun; that's okay too. It's okay to be picky about the person you're going to spend the most time with! If you're in a relationship because it's comfortable, then you're not leaving room for something better to come along. The solitude can be scary, but it's totally worth it in the end. I promise. Plus, so much growth happens when we explore on our own!

Lesson 14
Keep Going!

Falling down is all part of the journey. It is how we grow and learn. But often, we're so afraid to fail that we don't even try. Not even going for it, whatever IT is to you? To me, that's the ultimate failure.

Then, when we do try and we end up falling short of success, we beat ourselves up! Do we do that to little kids? Imagine a little kid is running a race and they fall down. Does a parent go, "Yeah! Stay down!" and spit at them?

No! Hopefully, if you're a good parent, you go, "Get up! You can do it! You can do it!" And the kid runs and kills it. Right? But when we're adults and we "fall down" while working toward a goal, we're so mean to ourselves. We all need to stop that! That definitely doesn't help and only keeps us from moving forward sooner. We have to be so, so kind to ourselves. There's always tomorrow. We don't need these insanely high expectations. And not meeting the expectations we have of ourselves doesn't mean anything. It doesn't mean that we're not good enough. We just have to keep going until we accomplish our goal.

Take writing this book, for instance. I've wanted to write one for so long, but I always felt too busy to find the time. Then, one day, I just started. Some days I got stuck, but I persevered and got it done. Little victories over time is how we win the war for success. Wars can't be won in one day. Move forward with love and compassion. It's all an inside job, and what we say to ourselves is most important. Let's encourage ourselves to keep going today!

Lesson 15
Honest Check-In!

Guess who's feeling rage today? I am! I am! It's because I haven't moved at all. This coronavirus quarantine has me all cooped up in the house, and I want to get out and see more than the area around my neighborhood and backyard.

Again, motion affects emotion. Moving regularly can combat irritability. If I'm not getting movement and my morning gratitude walks, how do you think my day is going to go? Not great. It won't be long until I'm restless, irritable, and discontent. After my exercise or my dancing session, if I'm still feeling a little bit emotional, I'll write a letter to explore all of the things that might be upsetting me.

We need to take the time to check in with ourselves and ask ourselves what it is we really need. And for me, in this moment, I crave connection. I'd like to get out and socialize with friends and family that I'm not getting a chance to see. (I'll FaceTime since I'm quarantined.) If we don't get honest about how we're really feeling, then we can't fix or change it.

So, check in with yourself after this. Ask yourself what's bothering you and what would make you happy. Maybe jot down some steps you can take to better your situation.

Lesson 16
Just Show Up!

There are so many things in life that can be scary or intimidating. Fear is what causes us to get in our own way. But that's not what God, the Universe, or love wants us to do. Eckhart Tolle said it best with: "Always say "yes" to the present moment. What could be more futile, more insane, than to create inner resistance to what already is? What could be more insane than to oppose life itself, which is now and always now? Surrender to what is. Say "yes" to life—and see how life suddenly starts working for you rather than against you."

Sometimes all you need to do in this life is to say yes—to just show up. Our brains tend to want to try to figure things out before we venture out into something that we have no control over. We do that to avoid being taken advantage of or blindsided by the unexpected, because we're really just trying to protect ourselves. Future uncertainties are the source of anxiety. Well, I'm here to remind you that so much of the excitement in life is in the surprises!

So maybe figuring it all out in advance isn't our job. We're not supercomputers, after all. There's no way to accurately predict the probability of every single possibility stemming from each time we step out of our comfort zone. The point is, you don't have to know how it's going to work out, or why, or when. Maybe we can just start trusting that the right thing *will* happen and things *will* work out in our favor. And if they don't? Well, even the hardest times will pass, so why not go for it? Your job is to just show up and enjoy each experience that awaits you. Growth can't happen if we stay stagnant and comfortable.

Lesson 17
Gift Yourself Me-Time!

Whether you're more introverted or more extroverted, we all need a little bit of quiet time—time to ourselves. The world can be *very* busy. If you work in an office, you can always go to the bathroom if you're feeling a little bit stressed so you can just breathe. Get in touch with your five senses. Remember to be *here* now.

Oftentimes, we stress ourselves out by thinking about the future too much, and that can cause anxiety. Or we linger on the past, and that can cause depression. But when we're right here, right now, everything is all okay. You're allowed to take as much time as you need for yourself here in the now. You can't work if you aren't grounded. The ones who love you won't mind that you're taking space for yourself. Your life matters! Your wellness matters! Take that time for yourself, even if it's two minutes; it will change your day.

Let's make sure we are in self-care today and every day, because no one else can take care of us the way we take care of ourselves!

Lesson 18
Love Each Other!

I talk about love a lot because it is so very crucial to our survival. I already touched on loving yourself, but for this lesson, I'd like to focus on having loving energy to give.

I believe we are all connected, which is why when an angry man is yelling across the street, you don't just hear it; you can kind of feel it. And when we're rude to people, it hurts. It might feel good in the moment because we're letting out our pain, but ultimately, we want to *give* love and connection as much as we want to feel it. The way we treat others is the way that we're treating ourselves. Again, hurt people hurt people. So, we have to be very careful and delicate with how we treat each other.

What if we didn't need a reason to be super kind and loving to one another? What would the world look like if love was all there was? My guess is that it would probably be pretty magical! Let's remember to treat ourselves and others with love, whether or not it seems deserved.

Love is free. Love is abundant. Go out and be kind and loving today!

Lesson 19
Let Go of Trying So Hard!

This lesson gon' be lit. And I will tell you why. I've been wearing the same shirt for two days. My hair is still the way it was when I woke up, and I don't care. We need to stop giving a baker's dozen about the way we're perceived, because we'll never be able to actually know what other people are thinking about us. It's almost a wasted effort to even pretend to know what they are thinking.

I heard this saying once: "What other people think of you is none of your business!" And I love that.

Trying to make everyone like you is IMPOSSIBLE and takes way too much energy anyway. They're not all going to like you, so there's no point in wasting your energy on it. When we care too much about things, it leads us to get attached to a specific outcome. That actually blocks out any other fun possibilities that might otherwise come to fruition! I don't think living things like to feel chained to any one idea. I know I don't. I like feeling the possibilities of the world!

When we relax and take it easy, things flow to us much more easily. I know this from my own experience. When I allow the river of life to flow, I have more energy, because I'm letting the current take me rather than resisting and thinking I'm supposed to be going in the opposite direction.

And, honestly, if a person doesn't like you, that's them projecting *their* insecurities on *you*. Same goes for love. If someone tells you, "I love you," that's because they have love in their hearts for themselves and therefore have love available to give. *You* just bring it out of them. We are all special and none of us are special. So, take that pressure off.

It's not about you. Stop giving an eff! Just be who you are! Embrace it! Be free with it!

People like being around people who don't care and don't try so hard. Can't you feel when someone is really desperate to try and it's really off-putting? It's because they're not being authentic. So relax and be you today. And every day.

Let's give no Fudgsicles!

Lesson 20
Love the Parts of You That Hurt!

We all have emotional booboos. We just can't see them. What do I do when I get a cut to make it heal? First, I acknowledge that it's there. Next, I give it a little Neosporin, a little love. Then I wrap it up. I think that it's important that we do this for our emotional body too. Those wounds we can't see come out at different times. When they do, I suggest that you give them some love, because that's what they need.

So, to heal a broken heart, first, we have to acknowledge that it's there. Then we have to love the parts of ourselves that hurt. Loving the parts of you that hurt—that's what healing is. Not picking at them, not getting mad that sorrow, anger, or depression is there, but giving them loving attention and then going easy on them by avoiding things that might "infect" our emotional wounds and delay healing. Give them the time they need to heal. We all deserve to give ourselves the gift of time.

We need to be so, so gentle and kind to ourselves. That's why I always talk about giving yourself a hug. Because healing starts with *us* first.

Please read the following out loud: "I LOVE ME!"

Lesson 21
Clear Negativity!

A Buddhist master named Thich Nhat Hanh once said: "Buddhism teaches that joy and happiness arise from letting go. Please sit down and take an inventory of your life. There are things you've been hanging on to that really are not useful and deprive you of your freedom. Find the courage to let them go."

Positive thinking really *can* help you let go of all the negativity around you. The ego's favorite way of strengthening itself is by complaining. If you catch yourself complaining, just remember, you're feeding your ego mind, and it doesn't always serve us to be in our ego. We're dying to be in our hearts. Maybe you've heard the adage about how we all have two wolves in us—the good wolf, full of joy, peace, and love, and the evil wolf, filled with anger, jealousy, and ego. The wolf that lives is the one you feed. Where your attention goes, energy flows, so focus on the good. If you focus on the bad, that's what you will get more of. Instead, focus on what you have. Be grateful. Focus on the positive things you want to bring into your life. Soon enough the evil wolf will die.

If you have someone in your life who's negative, maybe give yourself some space from them every now and then. We need to protect ourselves. We are all so susceptible to input from the outside world! Every minute, we are unconsciously taking in so much information that unknowingly affects us. We need to purge as much negativity as we can and surround ourselves with more positivity.

Which social media accounts do you look at? The ones that make you feel good inside or the ones that don't? Even the media we consume can affect us. Let's be careful where we spend our energy and what we take in.

Lesson 22
Be Honest with Yourself!

I feel compelled to talk about honesty. If we don't have honesty with ourselves and with other people, how do we build trust? How do we really feel safe, taken care of? How do we know what's really going on? To me, feeling I can be honest with myself and others is one of the most important things to me. Sounds easy enough to do, but actually, many people fib because they don't feel good enough inside. People exaggerate or completely invent stories because I think we as humans feel like we aren't enough just being who we are. But the truth is, the stories don't matter, the details don't matter. What matters is that we are here on this planet, alive and breathing. Our presence is the real present, and if we can get in touch with who we really are and bring that… well, that's the real gift.

Whenever there's deceit in your heart, mind, or spirit, write it down on a piece of paper, see it, and ask yourself, *Why am I fabricating in this way? What is it that I don't think I'm doing enough of?* If you do that, I bet you some feelings will come up. Sit with those feelings. Feel them. Know that no matter where you are in life, the honest you *IS* enough. Once you realize that and admit to yourself what's really on your mind, you'll respect yourself more. And once you're honest with yourself, you'll find it's sooo much easier to be honest with those around you.

Lesson 23
Get a Morning Routine!

It's important to start your day with love and intention. If I start my day going straight to my phone and checking social media, I'll fall into the trap of comparing and despairing. For me, that's starting off on the wrong foot. Well, maybe not the *wrong* foot, but it's not a *great* start.

I start with prayer, meditation, quieting the mind for a few minutes. A cup or three of coffee is essential. HA! For ME. Me love coffee. Black! Then I write a little note that says "Every day, in every way, my life gets better and better." And reading that sets me up for having a really, really good day.

My mornings are my me-time. And we all deserve me-time! Really think about how you spend the first hour of your day. Is it frantic or is it quiet? For me, God is in the silence. But if I'm yelling, watching TV, or on social media, then things are not quiet enough for me to hear God or universal intelligence or whatever it is you believe in (there's no right or wrong there).

Start the day doing something that makes you happy so happiness may permeate throughout your whole day!

Lesson 24
You're Where You're Supposed to Be!

You are not a burden. Some of you may be like, "What? Yes, I am." No. No, you're not. We are all equal. We are all connected. We are all one. We are deserving. We are here on the planet. You are doing a great job. Just breathe. Fear is just excitement without the breath. Keep breathing. You are right where you need to be. If you don't like where you are, go somewhere else. Take action. Even if it's something really small, you'll feel better about your situation and take a step toward where you want to be.

I myself sometimes think that if I were just X, Y, or Z, then I would feel better. And unfortunately, if I were meant to be at some other stage of life right now, then I would be. If I were meant to have already accomplished whatever goal I want to reach, then I would have. Why don't we take a moment to breathe and appreciate where we are in this exact moment? Neighborhood gratitude walks and thinking about what I'm grateful for always help spark my mood and help me remember how much I have. Sometimes we forget how much better we have it than others who are less fortunate. Remind yourself how bad your life could be and be thankful for all that you have.

Lesson 25
No Pain, No Gain!

Grieving. Whether you're experiencing the loss of a job, a loved one, or a relationship, or past pain or trauma, it's appropriate to grieve. Feeling the pain is okay, even necessary. Pain is the touchstone of spiritual growth. If you ever feel like something hurts so bad and you're so fed up with it that you have to stop it this very moment, then the change happens. It's that moment when you realize that you have to quit drinking or smoking or when you realize you have to break up with someone. That's your body's way of saying, *"No more, this is not good for me."*

Even if you're dealing with the loss of someone you care about, you need to feel the pain of their absence. You do this by feeling it into your body. Cry it out, scream into a pillow, write a letter and then burn it. All these things are fine. Why do we judge ourselves so harshly? We need not do that. Whatever we feel we need to do to cope is perfectly acceptable, because it's all part of the process, and we don't want to skip a single step.

Pain is there to work for us, not against us. It's there to tell us to go easy. It's part of the process and is essential for healing. There are so many things in this life that we just brush past because we think we have to be strong. Feeling your pain and going through it *is* strength! Feel whatever you need to feel today. It will pass and get better because it always does.

Lesson 26
Leave It in the Past!

The word "depression" is used so often these days. Whether it's due to a circumstance or an event that's gotten us down, or a chemical imbalance, it just seems so common these days. Chances are you or someone you know is dealing with depression. If you think you might be dealing with a chemical imbalance, it's important to reach out to a medical professional for the right medicine—you can't help your genes, and there's no shame in getting help with any illness, mental or physical. But if you experience depression in response to something that's going on in your life, there's a technique that really helps me to move past it.

I have mentioned going on gratitude walks, meditating, praying, and focusing on what I have instead of what I don't have. These things help. But what really helps me get into a positive frame of mind is stating things as being in the past. Flag this page, because this is huge! The unconscious mind is like a five-year-old, and it takes things *very* literally. Let's say you're depressed. The first thing to focus on is your language about it. Language drives behavior, so what we say to ourselves is most important. Instead of saying, "I am depressed," try saying, "I used to be depressed."

"I used to drink."

"I used to be a binge eater."

Whatever problem you're dealing with, say that it's in the past. The mind will hear it and go, *"Oh, okay, if I'm not that, I'm something better. Now, what can the future be? Something different? Something better?"*

Again, depression (the non-biochemical kind) comes from dwelling on the past. Leave all of the negativity—all of those failed successes and could've-beens—in the past behind you. Don't dwell. Move forward. You're not gonna lose anything by trying this technique of saying out loud that negative things are in the past now. See what happens!

Lesson 27
Do What Makes You Nervous!

We MUST do the things that make us nervous because that's how we grow and learn. The reason we don't want to do those things is fear. Fear of failure. Fear of the unknown. But what if there is no failure, only feedback? Instead of thinking of each risk as something that might hurt, think of it as another potential teachable moment. Because that's what every experience is!

For a long time, I wouldn't even try things because I didn't want to fail, probably because sometime in, like, first grade or whatever I did my homework wrong and it was so painful that I said, "Forget it, I'm just going to give up! If I don't try, then I can't fail!"

But when the time comes that I am on my deathbed, I can either lie there filled with regret over all of the things that I didn't do, or I can find peace in all of the wonderful things I got to experience. Why would anyone want to face regret in the final moments instead of bliss? Because of fear? No, no… We're not going to let fear ruin our lives. If we're afraid of it, then we must do it. MUST! Not should. Not, "*Oh, maybe I will.*" Must.

Taking chances is what makes life fun! All we can do is try as many things as we can and give everything 110 percent! Let's go easy on ourselves and take risks and look as bad as possible so we no longer fear anything!

Lesson 28
Swap "Nervous" for "Excited"!

Let's talk about nerves, baby. Let's talk about what they do to me!

Nerves basically show up as fear and convince me that I probably shouldn't do the thing that my heart knows I want to do. I'm sure you can relate to that.

It's been suggested to me time and time again that I should exchange "I'm nervous" for "I'm excited," because apparently, the same points in the brain are triggered by both feelings. It's our perception that makes us feel one or the other. Also, fear is going to come and try to protect you from the uncertainty of whatever you're considering doing. But what I like to ask myself is, *How will I feel if I don't do this? How will I feel if I follow the fear instead of faith?* Any time I follow faith, it pays off. When I follow the fear, I have regrets. And I absolutely *CANNOT* live with regrets! Train yourself to be more regret averse than fear averse.

For me, once I know I'm afraid of something, I *HAVE* to do that thing so I can know that it won't kill me. Y'all feel me?

Another really helpful thing I've learned is that whatever I'm afraid of, whatever I'm questioning doing, always passes. Always. Whether it's an hour-long performance or a coffee date with someone, an interview, an audition—it's always going to pass. What really helps me is to picture the moment in the future when it's done. Because in the future, it's already over. That truly works for me, and I hope that helps you.

FACE YOUR FEAR! You can do it! Just remember, you are excited, not nervous!

Lesson 29
Meditate!

Problems will always be there; it's the way we look at them and interact with them that really matters. And meditation has been a powerful tool to help me deal with the many problems that keep cropping up in my life.

Years ago, I learned Vedic meditation, which involves meditating twenty minutes twice a day with a mantra. For the first year that I did it, wooooo, my life was problem free! For the most part. The things that were bothering me all just went away.

The ego will tell us that we don't need to meditate, that there's no time. That's the way the ego strengthens itself, by preventing us from having an opportunity to get a clear mind. I stopped meditating for a while, then when I picked it back up, the things that I thought were problems really weren't problems at all. That's what meditation does. It quiets the mind. It clears away the thoughts so that when we go out into the world, we're more present and less reactive, which is definitely the way I want to be in the world.

I recommend you try it. Put your phone in another room, find somewhere quiet, then follow your breath. In. Out. See how you feel after. You don't have to do twenty minutes twice a day. Maybe try doing five minutes in the morning or five minutes at night. Start small and keep building up if you find that it helps you.

Lesson 30
Do It Anyway!

Ignore the voice in your head telling you not to do that thing you want to do or that thing that you know will be good for you. Sometimes we let every little thought get in the way of our doing the thing that would make us feel good, like creating or writing.

Ugh, I don't have the energy to.

But I just laid down…

Maybe tomorrow…

Maybe there won't be a tomorrow. Another gem that Eckhart Tolle wrote is: "Time isn't precious at all, because it is an illusion. What you perceive as precious is not time but the one point that is out of time: the Now. That is precious indeed. The more you are focused on time—past and future—the more you miss the Now, the most precious thing there is." I try to remind myself of this every day. Remember it. Live it. Not for me, for you.

The now is all we have. The past is gone. The future is not promised. That voice speaking against what you want is not the voice you want to listen to. Just get up and do that thing that's calling out to you anyway!

ACKNOWLEDGMENTS

MAMA, thank you for birthing me and showing me love and kindness. Your beauty and grace will always light me up.

PAPA, your encouragement gave me the strength to keep following my dreams. I owe you my life!

DENNIS THOMPSON - there is NO way I could have done this without you. You MADE this happen. I am forever grateful for your hard work and for being available whenever I needed you. THANK YOU, THANK YOU, THANK YOU!

ELISA QUINZI - You rock star! You catapulted my life into spirituality and made me believe in taking the best care of myself. Thank you for all you've done for me. You know what it is!

TARA TOLOOEE - My BFF for life! You saved me in more ways than one. Thank you for inspiring me to keep being myself and for laughing at every joke… even when they weren't funny.

TRAVIS HARRIS - You are my brother from another mother! My love for you is unalterable. NO one can touch it. It is sacred to me and our friendship will surely last many lifetimes. Thanks for always making me laugh and for making me feel like I was special to you. Thank you for all the love you pass around. Thanks for being by myside all these years.

LAURA CLERY- My kindred spirit sister. You've inspired me in every way. You embody everything I want to be. I look up to you. I can talk to you about ANYTHING. You guided me through my recent heartbreak and made me feel worth it. I love you BEYOND WORDS.

LAURA ROBBINS- Thank you for being a huge role model for me. Thank you for being the first person to read my book and for your notes. Your kindness heals me! And thank you for the quote. TEEHEE

MY BDBS- You ladies are my tribe! I adore you all more than I can say. I cherish our time together and our phone check-ins. You are my heart, and I pray we continue on our journeys together for the rest of our days!

TO ALL OF MY FAMILY - I love you. You have all supported my dream, and that means everything to me. You have my love and support, always.

SHANNON CHAN KENT - Thanks for your humor and light. You came in like an Angel from heaven during the hardest time of my life. Thank you for listening and laughing. You're one of my favorite playmates!

HAL - Thank you for your constant humor and love.

THERESA – You're one of my biggest fans. I appreciate you more than you know. Thank you for loving my mother and loving me. You are my family. I hope to make you proud and be on SNL one day.

MY VINE CREW (Vincent Marcus, J. Cyrus, Matt Cutshall, Ry Doon, Jason Nash, Brandon Calvillo) - Creating with you boys will be in my heart forever. Countless hilarious times provided me with laughter fed my soul. I love that we have content from years ago that still makes me laugh to this day. What a blessed time to remember always.

HANNAH - I have learned SO much from our friendship. Thank you for the laughs and creativity you brought to my life.

MIKE CARSON - Your sense of humor always keeps me laughing. Thank you for teaching me how to be light. Keep it up. And thanks for being there for my papa!

PIEDAD - Thank you for loving my dad so dearly. I love you.

CENTA & RICHARD - you've been in my life forever and you've always taken such good care of my mother and me. I appreciate you.

NEW YORK CITY – You've changed me in many ways and opened up my life tenfold. I can't wait to see and experience you again.

RUSSELL - YOU ARE MY SON, MY MOST PRIZED. I love you more than ANYTHING. Thank you for keeping me happy.

JONNY CARLSON- Hey, SAWEETY! I appreciate all you do. You made me laugh during a time that I didn't feel like laughing.

TO ALL OF MY FOLLOWERS- YOU MADE THIS HAPPEN! WITHOUT YOU, I wouldn't be here, I wouldn't have written a book. I wouldn't have kept creating in the way I do. You keep me going! I see you. I hear you. I love you. THANK YOU!

Need More Manon?

Subscribe to <u>ManonMathews.com</u> For:

●Merch●

●Laughs●

●Motivation●

@ManonMathews

CPSIA information can be obtained
at www.ICGtesting.com
Printed in the USA
BVHW030155080720
583235BV00005B/17/J